MACMILLAN MASTER GUIDES

THE MILL ON THE FLOSS BY GEORGE ELIOT

HELEN WHEELER

First edition 1986

Published by
MACMILLAN EDUCATION LTD
Houndmills, Basingstoke, Hampshire RG21 2XS
and London
Companies and representatives
throughout the world

Typeset by
TecSet, Sutton, Surrey
Printed in Hong Kong

British Library Cataloguing in Publication Data
Wheeler, Helen
The Mill on the Floss by George Eliot. –
(Macmillan master guides)
1. Eliot, George. Mill on the Floss
I. Title
823′.8 PR4664
ISBN 0-333-40589-7 Pbk
ISBN 0-333 40590-8 Pbk export

CONTENTS

General editor's preface		vii
Acknowledgements		
1 George Eliot: life in relation to *The Mill on the Floss*	1.1 Prologue: why four names?	1
	1.2 Relevance of biographical elements	3
	1.3 Where Mary Ann is not Maggie	7
	1.4 *The Mill on the Floss* in relation to Eliot's other novels	9
2 *The Mill on the Floss*	2.1 A guide to St Ogg's	10
	2.2 Time in *The Mill on the Floss*	11
3 Summaries and critical commentary	3.1 General summary	15
	3.2 Chapter summaries and critical commentary	16
4 Themes and issues	4.1 Romantic fascination with the child	52
	4.2 The duty of the artist: the impossibility of moral judgements	56
	4.3 *The Mill on the Floss* as social history	57
	4.4 The individual and society	58
	4.5 Religious climate	59
	4.6 Scientific ideas	61
	4.7 The position of women	64
5 Style and technique	5.1 Dialect	66
	5.2 The authorial voice	67
	5.3 Varieties of style	68
	5.4 Character and plot	70
	5.5 The problem of ending	72
	5.6 Images and reality	73
6 Critical analysis	6.1 Approach	76
	6.2 Specimen passage and critical commentary	77

7 Critical reception	7.1 Contemporary reviews and reactions	82
	7.2 Subsequent history of the book	84
Revision questions		85
Further reading		86

GENERAL EDITOR'S PREFACE

The aim of the Macmillan Master Guides is to help you to appreciate the book you are studying by providing information about it and by suggesting ways of reading and thinking about it which will lead to a fuller understanding. The section on the writer's life and background has been designed to illustrate those aspects of the writer's life which have influenced the work, and to place it in its personal and literary context. The summaries and critical commentary are of special importance in that each brief summary of the action is followed by an examination of the significant critical points. The space which might have been given to repetitive explanatory notes has been devoted to a detailed analysis of the kind of passage which might confront you in an examination. Literary criticism is concerned with both the broader aspects of the work being studied and with its detail. The ideas which meet us in reading a great work of literature, and their relevance to us today, are an essential part of our study, and our Guides look at the thought of their subject in some detail. But just as essential is the craft with which the writer has constructed his work of art, and this may be considered under several technical headings – characterisation, language, style and stagecraft, for example.

The authors of these Guides are all teachers and writers of wide experience, and they have chosen to write about books they admire and know well in the belief that they can communicate their admiration to you. But you yourself must read and know intimately the book you are studying. No one can do that for you. You should see this book as a lamp-post. Use it to shed light, not to lean against. If you know your text and know what it is saying about life, and how it says it, then you will enjoy it, and there is no better way of passing an examination in literature.

JAMES GIBSON

ACKNOWLEDGEMENTS

Cover illustration: *The Miller's Boat*
by Frederick Richard Lee, © Guildhall
Art Gallery and by courtesy of the
Bridgeman Art Library.

1 GEORGE ELIOT: LIFE IN RELATION TO *THE MILL ON THE FLOSS*

1.1 PROLOGUE: WHY FOUR NAMES?

Mary Ann Evans (or Marian, or Polly)

Our author was christened Mary Ann in 1819 after two of her mother's sisters and so was known officially as Mary Ann Evans through childhood and girlhood, and unofficially as Polly. Her baptismal certificate has 'Mary Anne' but her father's diary calls her 'Ann' and she used this form after 1837. No name at all appeared on her first published book, the 1846 translation of Strauss's *Life of Jesus*, but when she translated *The Essence of Christianity* by Feuerbach in 1854, the name Marian Evans was on the title-page – the only time this happened. She had adopted the new form of her Christian name, Marian, in her letters, after her return in 1850 from an eight-month visit to Switzerland.

Mrs Lewes

In July 1854, she and the writer George Henry Lewes decided to live together, a course of action both highly unusual at this time and courageous. They could not marry: Lewes was already married, though his wife had been living for some time with another man by whom she had had three children. Lewes had once received her back after her first infidelity, and so English law would never allow him to divorce her. In an 1857 letter Marian said, 'our marriage is not a legal one, though it is regarded by us both as a sacred bond . . . ' and that since their union she 'had borne his name'. In another letter she wrote, 'the few friends who are about me should recognise me as Mrs Lewes'. Most did, but it is typical that Mrs Gaskell, another novelist who never met her, but immensely admired her work, felt bound to say, 'I wish you *were* Mrs Lewes'.

George Eliot

In 1857, the first novel (in fact it is three long stories), *Scenes of Clerical Life*, appeared. It was foolhardy for a woman to start publication under her own name and impossible for Marian Evans/Mrs Lewes whose rejection of a conventional life-style had already attracted furious attack. So she chose yet another name: George Eliot. The origin of the first is obvious, specially as it was George Henry Lewes's encouragement that had first led her to attempt writing fiction; the second, 'Eliot', she explained as 'a good, mouth-filling, easily pronounced word'. But there may be other reasons: the initial of her own surname is preserved, and Elliott is the name which the heroine chooses to conceal her real identity in Charlotte Brontë's novel *Jane Eyre*.

To her chosen pseudonym she clung, long after the real identity of the writer was known: George Eliot became the name by which the vast majority of her readers think of her as a novelist and as a person, so that it is with a slight jolt that we focus on whom G. H. Lewes is talking about when, for instance, he writes in his journal that he 'danced with Polly to warm her feet'.

Mary Ann Cross

Lewes died in 1878, and in May 1880 Marian married John Walter Cross. She reverted to her baptismal Mary Ann: her signature now was Mary Ann Cross. The marriage was brief – by December 1880 she was dead.

It is typical of the confusion surrounding her names that just before her funeral in Highgate cemetery, a friend of hers was asked by a waiting child if it was the late George Eliot's wife who was going to be buried. Inevitably, too, there is confusion for the student: 'George Eliot' suggests the established, world-famous novelist and carries an inevitable suggestion of confident masculinity. Yet the George Eliot persona only came into existence when Mary Ann Evans was already thirty-seven years old, with an unusually successful career as translator and literary journalist behind her. Moreover, no other great English woman novelist has been so permanently concealed in this way: Jane Austen quickly emerged from anonymity and the Brontës from their androgynous pseudonyms. This oddly prolonged dissimulation has always been a problem to biographers. Nothing could be more unsuitable than, for instance, to identify the stolidly successful name of George Eliot with what she herself called the 'absolute despair' of her early years and specially with *The Mill on the Floss* which reflects this experience most keenly.

In order to balance this identification and to simplify biographical references, the brief Eliot will be used throughout this book.

1.2 RELEVANCE OF BIOGRAPHICAL ELEMENTS

The Mill on the Floss is Eliot's third novel and the most openly autobiographical she was ever to write. She herself said she was exploring her 'remotest past', so the novel has the added interest of suggesting interconnections between a work of art and its sources. Knowledge of her own life enlarges our understanding of her fictional *alter ego*, young Maggie Tulliver, of the relationships within the novel and of its structure. Some of the elements which connect fiction and reality are explicit, others much more disguised, some only conjectural.

Childhood in the country

Eliot's childhood was spent in the Warwickshire countryside at a farmhouse near Griff and the memory of the lovely old house, its orchards, gardens, farmyard, Round Pool and the nearby Arbury Mill haunted her for the rest of her life. Maggie's childhood establishes the same deep imprint: 'the thoughts and loves of these first years would always make part of their lives . . . These familiar flowers, these well-remembered bird notes, this sky with its fitful brightness, these furrowed and grassy fields . . . are the mother tongue of our imagination' (Book 1, Chapter 5). The easy changeover in this passage from third to first person establishes the close relationship between fiction and reality. But much as Eliot loved the country, she had no idyllic illusions about the quality of country life. In an 1856 article she speaks of the need to understand 'the peasant in all his coarse apathy and the artisan in his suspicious selfishness' and there is nothing romantic or sentimental in her treatment of gypsies, or of the Dodson clan ('stingy, selfish wretches' said *The Times*'s reviewer). Like Maggie, Eliot lived in the heart of provincial England where change was reluctant and unusual aspirations received little sympathy. The reaction of St Ogg's to Maggie's misadventure vividly reflects Eliot's own experience of such censoriousness.

Parentage

The Evans family was much more complicated than the Tullivers, since Robert Evans married twice and had five children altogether, two by his first wife and then Chrissey (born 1814), Isaac (1816), and finally Mary Ann (1819). Her father was (unlike Mr Tulliver) a highly successful estate manager who had risen to that position from being a carpenter. Obviously a man of great natural ability and strength, he yet 'had a certain self-distrust, owing perhaps to his early imperfect education' (John Cross's *Life*). If this is true, it would fit in with his increasing suspicion of his clever young daughter, and when she lost her faith in 1842 (at this time she was acting as housekeeper to her widowed father) he was outraged and refused to have her live with him. Superficially the breach was healed: Eliot compromised and went on accompanying her father to church; she looked after the old man until he died in May 1849 and she herself was twenty-nine.

There are obvious affinities between Mr Tulliver and Robert Evans and echoes of the real father's illness and death in the novel. The conflict between Eliot and her father interestingly shifts on to Tom's assumption of authority and Maggie's challenge of this; her painful feeling of emotional and intellectual isolation within her family, however, clearly stems from her experience. In the novel, Mr Tulliver's devotion to 'his little wench' is one of his most attractive traits and no friction is allowed to disturb it. When Eliot was a child she often went on business rounds with her father, standing between his knees in the gig 'while he rode leisurely' but there is no evidence of special fondness from her father later in life: the vivid presentation of Mr Tulliver's protective and admiring affection suggests how much Eliot would have liked this to be true of her own girlhood.

Eliot's mother only resembled Mrs Tulliver in two ways: she preferred her son and she had three married sisters whose ideas of what was 'customary and respectable' were going to be patterns for the Dodsons. She certainly sent her daughters off to boarding school very promptly – like her elder sister, Eliot went at five years old. Perhaps this has something to do with the scarcity of good mother-daughter relationships in the novels. Mrs Tulliver seems to inhabit a different world from Maggie and the reader is astonished by the one moment when she comes to her aid (Book 7, Chapter 1). She very quickly retreats again into 'poor aunt Tulliver, that no-one made any account of' and is unmentioned in the conclusion.

Brother Isaac and Brother Tom: the hunger for love

Eliot's nature was warmly affectionate, with what John Cross later described as 'the absolute need of some one person to whom she should be all in all'. In her earliest years she put her brother Isaac in this place and they were inseparable companions until he was eight and went off to school. He was never really her playmate again, since he spent his holidays in riding and other outdoor sports, so she had to make do with just the books that Maggie would have: John Bunyan's *Pilgrim's Progress*, Daniel Defoe's *History of the Devil*, and later on, the novels of Sir Walter Scott. It is typical of their divergence of interests that when they visited London together in 1838, he bought her Josephus's *History of the Jews*, but for himself (at the same shop), a couple of sporting prints. Years later, in 1869, Eliot wrote a sonnet sequence, *Brother and Sister*, in which she recalls the intense emotion of this childish relationship, her adoration and obedience:

> If he said 'Hush!', I tried to hold my breath,
> Wherever he said 'Come!' I stepped in faith

and sees in these years the seed-time of her soul:

> The fear, the love, the primal passionate store,
> Whose shaping impulses make manhood whole.

Among these shaping impulses, a fishing expedition is described at some length, her terror of her brother's anger when her dreaminess puts the line in danger and the successful outcome. The reader of *The Mill on the Floss* recognises the incident at once and the conflicting temperaments of the two children.

In adult life Isaac became increasingly disapproving of his sister's independence of mind and unconventional ways. In typical Victorian style he regarded himself after his father's death as head of the family and had quarrelled with his sister even before she set up her unorthodox household with Lewes – a step which made him sever communication with her completely until her legal marriage to Cross twenty-six years later.

Maggie's dog-like devotion to Tom and his cooler attitude to her obviously derive from Eliot's own childhood, and the feelings of guilt which Tom inspires in his sister mirror the conflict between the prosaic, conventional, authoritarian Isaac and his highly intelligent but emotionally vulnerable sister. Other aspects are more debatable: it has been suggested that the structure of the book is finally unsatisfactory in that Maggie's frustrations are abruptly and melodramatically resolved in terms only of her relationship to Tom – to the surprise of the reader who has been following Maggie along a different path that had left childhood far behind. The novel, that is, exorcises Eliot's broken relationship with her once adored brother but leaves her reader nonplussed in that it bypasses her adult problems – the conflicting loyalties to Stephen, Philip, Lucy and, indeed, herself.

The experience of love

After her father's death Eliot spent nearly a year in Switzerland, lodging with the D'Alberts, who treated her with great kindness, Monsieur D'Albert painting her portrait. He was a very intelligent man who had been crippled by a boyhood accident. Eliot obviously felt considerable affection for him and for his wife: they corresponded for the rest of her life and he translated four of her novels into French. He may well have suggested some of the characteristics of Philip Wakem and he certainly appeared in her life at a time when, like Maggie, she desperately needed supportive kindness, after the death of her father and Isaac's coldness. In 1850 she returned to England and soon settled in London, becoming the assistant editor of the *Westminster Review*, a liberal intellectual journal edited by John Chapman. For some time she lodged in his house - 142, Strand. This was a typically Victorian set-up with the publishing and bookselling business on the ground floor and the Chapmans living above and letting rooms to lodgers. Less typical was the presence in the house of John Chapman's mistress, Elizabeth Tilley, who also acted as governess to the children and the emotional complications were considerably increased by Eliot's powerful presence. At this time Chapman was twenty-nine and, it is said, a very handsome man - it is probable that it was he who gave her that experience of impulsive physical attraction which Maggie feels for Stephen Guest.

At this house Eliot met many people of intellectual and artistic note in London, such as Charles Dickens and Charles Darwin. Among them was a philosopher and journalist, Herbert Spencer. A close friendship developed, but he was a curiously cold, self-centred man, who let it be known that love for him was impossible without great personal beauty. Eliot's letters at this time have repeated dispirited references to what she saw as her own ugliness: 'I am a hideous hag now', 'haggard as an old witch'. Much later the novelist, Henry James, described her as 'magnificently ugly . . . and horse faced' but immediately added that this was speedily forgotten because of her 'potent' charm. The hurt which she suffered from her lack of conventional mid-Victorian beauty was a deep one. *Jane Eyre* had set the fashion in 1847 for plain heroines, but the contrast between Maggie and Lucy goes deeper than this. When Maggie pushes Lucy into the mud, there is an element of revenge for all the unfair attraction that doll-like, fair-haired prettiness has ever exercised and in this case, on Tom. The pattern is intellectualised in Maggie's conversation with Philip about the sufferings of dark-haired heroines in novels, and repeated at a considerably deeper level later in the book when Maggie, now metamorphosed into 'startling beauty', wins Stephen away from her conventionally-pretty cousin.

By 1854 Eliot had at last found someone to be 'all in all' to her. This was George Henry Lewes whom she had met a few years before. The fact that they could not get married officially (section 1.1) seemed to them immaterial. External conventions meant nothing compared with 'a truly moral marriage . . . spontaneously willed'. In confiding their plan to live together to trusted friends, Eliot emphasised that their union could hurt no one, since Lewes's wife would never return to him and he would continue to support her and the children. It is useful here to recall Eliot's condemnation of Charlotte Brontë's heroine, Jane Eyre, who abandons Rochester when she finds he already has an incurably insane wife that he cannot divorce because of the 'diabolical' marriage law. In the event, the Lewes's union was a singularly happy and fruitful one, each partner supporting the other, Lewes in particular giving Eliot the self-confidence to embark upon writing novels.

Their union puts into perspective several aspects of *The Mill on the Floss*. It underlies the poignancy of Maggie's quest for someone to satisfy her 'need of being loved'. On the other hand, it emphasises under what circumstances such natural feelings, however powerful, must be resisted. Maggie's motivation in rejecting Stephen is that their marriage would destroy both Lucy and Philip. 'I cannot take a good for myself that has been wrung out of their misery' she says, and the contemporary reader is meant to realise how different was the moral decision that she and Lewes could take. Yet the novel's conclusion is elusive - what would have happened if there had been no flood? - and the possibility is left open that Dr Kenn may be justified in thinking of 'ultimate marriage between Stephen and Maggie as the least evil'.

There is a third connection between the Eliot/Lewes union and *The Mill on the Floss*. Though both were aware there would be scandal, they had moved so long among atypical, free-thinking Victorians that she, at least, was unprepared for the violence of disapproval, with its sanctimonious, indignant or jealous voices that their action aroused. It was the energy and ingenuity of both London and provincial gossip that inspired the chapter 'St Ogg's Passes Judgment' (Book 7, Chapter 2) where the tumultuous effect of many voices speaking in eloquent condemnation is balanced by a fastidious, distancing irony.

1.3 WHERE MARY ANN IS NOT MAGGIE

Education

Eliot's education was totally unlike Maggie's. She was at boarding schools from the age of five to seventeen, and when she returned home to look after her father she had visiting tutors: she could read French, German, Italian, Greek and Latin and later learnt Hebrew. She read widely in philosophy, science and theology, and became a good and enthusiastic pianist and singer.

Friends, religious position, literary career

Naturally this unusually clever girl attracted attention, and when her father moved house to Coventry she came to know Charles and Caroline Bray, an enlightened free-thinking pair. Through them she met well-known people like Robert Owen, the factory reformer, and Ralph Waldo Emerson, the American poet and philosopher, and became intimate with Sara Hennell, a highly educated and liberally-minded teacher, with whom she talked of everything under the sun. Her brother Charles Hennell had published in 1838 an *Inquiry concerning the Origin of Christianity*, 'one of the first attempts to regard Christianity from a purely historical point of view and separate it from all that was obviously legendary and mythical'. This was Charles Bray's description and the book which Eliot had already come across, was obviously much discussed in the Bray/Hennell circle. Through the Hennells she received her first commission, which was to translate from the German a recent, controversial life of Christ by the biblical scholar, David Strauss.

All these influences weaned Eliot away from the puritanically evangelical phase of her adolescence when, she later confessed, she went about 'like an owl'. Another influence was that of the novelist Sir Walter Scott, whose 'healthy and historical views' would, she found, not fit her narrow creed. Soon she rejected traditional Christianity altogether (hence the row with her father: see section 1.2) and did so with a feeling of enfranchisement, turning with relief to a tolerant humanism. By 1854, she had translated two of the most influential theological books of her time (see section 4.5) and was at the centre of London's intellectual life. By 1858 she had embarked upon a supremely successful career as a novelist.

'Poor Maggie'

Maggie is introduced to the reader as a particularly bright child, and her interest in Mr Stelling's lessons confirms her father's pride. Yet her development is stunted by the paucity of books (this is emphasised several times), the mere two years at boarding school, her deprivation of that pleasant enlargement of mind which comes from talking to intelligent and kindly friends and of the emotional release brought by art (music is limited to the church organ on Sundays). No wonder Philip and his offer of books are irresistible - as will be Stephen's music. Maggie's religious development is at once less narrow and less liberal than her creator's. Instead of becoming a rather fanatical Evangelical, she is influenced by the much sweeter self-renunciation of the mediaeval mystic, Thomas à Kempis. And since it would be most unlikely that St Ogg's would be touched by the unsettling influence of modern biblical scholarship, Maggie's faith is untroubled - it is moral, not theological doubts that she has to solve.

Another great difference between Eliot and Maggie concerns what might loosely be called 'the scientific approach'. When Maggie first meets Stephen Guest she is fascinated by his account of the Bridgewater Treatises. She becomes 'absorbed in his wonderful geological story'. This is probably the first time that she has encountered, in any way, nineteenth-century science, and it is typical that her reaction is fascinated rather than enquiring. Painfully, over the years, Eliot had acquired that special ability to absorb the scientific reliance on evidence and experiment into her own understanding of history, of society and of psychology. The ability for such an approach, with its consequent objectivity is totally unknown to the emotional, precipitate Maggie. Perhaps this is why Eliot displays such compassionate yearning towards her creation: she is repeatedly 'poor Maggie', 'poor child'.

1.4 *THE MILL ON THE FLOSS* IN RELATION TO ELIOT'S OTHER NOVELS

Eliot's early fiction is rooted firmly in provincial life and gains its power from the intimate knowledge of the people and places of her childhood, her ability to exploit the natural speech of the Midlands, from the way she could invest commonplace life and domestic details with complex significance and from her uncanny understanding of human motivation. *Scenes from Clerical Life* (1858) and *Adam Bede* (1859) build on these strengths, the latter particularly combining a pastoral richness and dignity, with a totally credible infanticide, and the splendidly edgy idiom of Mrs Poyser, a farmer's wife. Then comes *The Mill on the Floss* (1860) which develops within the provincial setting a consciousness of social and economic change, as well as a moving portrayal of childhood largely drawn from Eliot's own, while the language and eccentricities of Tullivers and Dodsons give realism to this narrow, middle-class society.

Silas Marner (1861) retains the country setting but has none of the tense and passionate unhappiness of its predecessor. The life of a miserly weaver is transformed by a baby girl being left on his doorstep and the book has a fairy-tale-cum-Wordsworthian quality though – as always in an Eliot novel – the duty of right moral choice provides an inexorable structure. *Romola* (1863) is set in the fifteenth-century Florence of the religious reformer, Savonarola, and is chiefly remembered for the meticulous scholarship of its background. *Felix Holt* (1866) is, like *The Mill on the Floss*, a novel about the 1830s, but has a strong political interest. *Middlemarch* (1871–2) is Eliot's masterpiece. It returns firmly to provincial society but explores it on many more levels than earlier novels. However, the subtle interplay of characters, the differentiation of idiom, the stunting of personality by environment, the insistence on moral choice and the disentangling of motive all recall St Ogg's. The final novel is *Daniel Deronda* (1876) an uneasy combination of the story of a disastrous marriage and of Zionism. Its links with *The Mill on the Floss* are the careful study of a woman's nature – Gwendolen Harleth – and the use of music as a pervasive metaphor.

2 THE MILL ON THE FLOSS

2.1 A GUIDE TO ST OGG'S

St Ogg's, a prosperous little trading town, lies on the confluence of the Rivers Ripple and Floss. Dorlcote Mill draws its water-power from the former, and the latter carries a busy boat trade from the wharves of St Ogg's to Mudport 15 miles away where the Floss reaches the North Sea. We hear that Stephen visits Holland and Tom Newcastle, but the novel does not follow them there. Maggie spends one night in York, but otherwise the novel is firmly centred round St Ogg's and Dorlcote Mill, the only exception being Tom's schooldays.

At Dorlcote Mill live Mr and Mrs Tulliver and their two children, Tom and Maggie. Tullivers have been millers and maltsters there for five generations. Kezia is their domestic servant and Luke, the head miller, lives with his wife in a nearby cottage. Mr Tulliver has one sister, Gritty, who is married to an unsuccessful farmer, Mr Moss. They live some miles away in the neglected parish of Basset, have eight children and owe Mr Tulliver £300.

Mrs Tulliver (Bessie) is the youngest of the four Dodson sisters, representatives of a family of good standing in the town for generations. All are now married. Jane, the eldest, is married to Mr Glegg, a retired woolstapler, a kindly man keen on gardening and nearly as thrifty as his wife. They live right in the centre of St Ogg's, with the front window looking down the Tofton Road and the garden stretching back to the river. They are childless. The second sister, Sophy, is the wife of Mr Pullet, a gentleman farmer. They live a little way out of St Ogg's on a pretty estate called Garum Firs. They, too, have no children. Mrs Pullet is inordinately house-proud and fascinated by her own and other people's ill-health.

The third sister, Susan, has married a man of business, Mr Deane, who has risen from a humble position in the firm of Guest & Co. (the most important trading house in St Ogg's) to a partnership. They have one child,

Lucy, and live in a pleasant house alongside the river in St Ogg's within walking distance of the Gleggs. Mrs Deane dies during the novel.

The lawyer Wakem is a widower and lives with his only legitimate child, Philip, in a 'handsome house' in Tofton, very near St Ogg's and also near an attractive wooded and slightly hilly area called the Red Deeps. On the other side of this is Dorlcote Mill.

The Guest family – father, two Miss Guests who are regarded as the 'glass of fashion by St Ogg's' and Stephen – live in Park House, the most imposing residence in the neighbourhood. The Guests own the 'largest oil mill and most extensive wharf' in St Ogg's and are considered very wealthy.

Dr Kenn comes as vicar to St Ogg's while Maggie is away teaching: his wife dies soon after Maggie's return. There are several children. Bob Jakin, when a boy, worked as a bird-scarer for Mr Tulliver; he becomes a successful pedlar and owns a house right on the Floss where he and his wife let lodgings. Riley, the auctioneer and valuer, lives at Mudport. He acts for Tulliver in water-right controversies, has several daughters and dies owing Tulliver money. It is Riley who suggests the Reverend Mr Stelling as a schoolmaster for Tom. The Stellings live at King's Norton, about fifteen miles from St Ogg's. He takes pupils to augment his curate's income and it is at his house that Tom and Maggie will get to know Philip Wakem.

Among characters referred to, but who do not appear in the novel, are Gore (Tulliver's lawyer), Pivart (his adversary in the law suit), Furley (who holds a mortgage on the Mill), and Jetsome (Wakem's illegitimate son whom he puts into Dorlcote Mill after Tulliver's death).

2.2 TIME IN *THE MILL ON THE FLOSS*

Variety of pace

Time operates at different tempos throughout the novel, sometimes subjective, sometimes with the objectivity of clock time. Many of the episodes are presented in what might be called dramatic time – that is, the scene could easily transfer to the stage. We are shown the characters in a particular setting, watch their movements, listen to what they say and note the effect on the hearer or a significant silence. The three scenes between Maggie and Philip in the Red Deeps (Book 5) are of this kind. But we must remember that these scenes are selected from others which Eliot leaves the reader to imagine from the way Maggie has changed, for between chapters 3 and 4 'nearly a year has elapsed'. Sometimes she devotes four chapters to a single day (Book 1, Chapters 8–11) but then lets two years go unchronicled. Tom's appearance to Maggie as a pirate is given a meticulously exact background from the first mention of Poulter, the drilling master, with his gin-inspired tales of the Peninsular War, to the final abortive sword-exercise – yet Maggie's two-year sojourn with Lucy at boarding school rates the briefest mention and no episode from Tom's life at work is presented first-hand.

Sometimes time slows down almost to a stop – for Maggie sobbing in the attic (Book 1, Chapters 5, 7) time is subjective: five minutes seem like hours and the same sense of timelessness overcomes her when she is drifting down river with Stephen – 'the past and future' are 'excluded'. Time can alter in this way for Tom as well, when he first realises the bleak difficulties of earning money. The two-hour visit to his uncle (Book 5, Chapter 5) alters his whole perspective of the future. Book 4 is, apart from its opening, divorced from any feeling of clock time, since it is a chronicle of interior rather than exterior life and this timeless effect is intensified, not only by Maggie's impression of hearing the voice of Thomas à Kempis from mediaeval times, but also by the glosses in her copy by the long-dead 'old brown hand'.

The oscillation between present time, in which there is even opportunity to notice Mr Tulliver thoughtfully stroking his woollen stockings, and a much longer time scheme manifests itself in several ways. One is by the use of memory – what the French novelist, Marcel Proust, called 'the inseparableness of us from the past'. Maggie and Tom can never forget their childhood, and the last sentence of Book 7 underlines this; Philip will never forget meeting little Maggie at school; his father recalls the face of his long-dead wife Emily. Mrs Tulliver remembers every detail to do with choosing her beloved household treasures, Mr Tulliver remembers the day the malting house was finished and how his father loved planting trees and thinks back through the generations of Tullivers who have lived at Dorlcote Mill. But the author takes us much further back even than this, into history and prehistory so that the lives of Tom and Maggie are seen under an overarching span of time. It is typical that the novel opens with the effect of a camera panning in from undefined time to a particular moment, and ends with a conclusion which can only look uncertainly and hesitantly into the future.

The eighteenth-century novelist, Henry Fielding, promised his reader 'when any extraordinary scene presents itself . . . we shall spare no pains to open it at large to our readers, but if whole years should pass without producing anything worthy his notice, we shall not be afraid of a chasm in our history, but shall hasten onto matters of consequence.' What the student must consider is why Eliot selects and why she rejects as she does: what, in fact, she knows to be 'of consequence'.

The happenings in the novel are held firmly in an exactly constructed cradle of time, while Maggie and Tom grow from children to young adults. The following time scheme maps out this chronology.

Time scheme

The opening of the novel is set some thirty years before the date of writing. References to the Duke of Wellington and Catholic Emancipation place this as February 1829. The Tullivers have been married for thirteen years and Tom and Maggie would have been born in 1816 and 1819 (the same years as Isaac Evans and his sister). So the chronology of the book works out like this:

Book 1: February 1829: the action is condensed into a brief period with, for instance, Mr Tulliver's visit to his sister, the rest of the family going to Garum Firs and Maggie's flight to the gypsies all happening on the same day.

Book 2: Midsummer 1829, when Tom first goes to school until November 1832 when Maggie arrives with the news of their father's loss of the law suit and subsequent stroke, and Tom leaves school for good.

Book 3: November 1832 until January or February 1833: this encompasses Tulliver's illness, the sale of the mill and its contents, Tom starting at Guest & Co. and the appointment of Tulliver as Wakem's employee. The book ends with the entry in the family Bible of Mr Tulliver's vow of revenge.

Book 4: The chestnut trees are out so we know the month is May, but the time is not further defined: Maggie's religious awakening and her subsequent attempts at self-conquest are intentionally left undated to suit the gradual growth of her spiritual self.

Book 5: June 1836–April 1837. This book opens with Maggie's first re-encounter with Philip when he is '4 or 5 years older' than Maggie – that is, he is twenty-two and Maggie is seventeen. It ends with Tom's discovery and ending of his sister's relationship with Philip, his repayment of his father's debts, the latter's attack on Wakem and own death the following day. All these events are condensed into four weeks.

Book 6: Spring to Summer 1839. Maggie has returned on a visit to St Ogg's after two years away. This book spans the three months of Stephen and Maggie's love affair and culminates in the disastrous river voyage and their parting.

Book 7: August to mid-September 1839: from Maggie's return to St Ogg's until the night of the great flood and the death of brother and sister.

Conclusion: 'Five years after' – but the dating is both exact as in this phrase and vague as in 'but that was years after'.

3 SUMMARIES AND CRITICAL COMMENTARY

3.1 GENERAL SUMMARY

The Mill on the Floss, set in the years 1829–39, centres on Maggie and Tom, children of the honest and respectable, but uneducated miller, Mr Tulliver, and his wife. An important peripheral group of characters includes Mrs Tulliver's three sisters and their husbands: two of these also exemplify the narrow provincialism of the trading town of St Ogg's while the third uncle, Mr Deane, is an enterprising business man able to offer Tom a job when his father ruins himself financially. This ruin stems from his generosity, unwise expenditure on Tom's education and, above all, his passion for litigation about his water-rights. After four years' grinding work and some help from a loyal childhood friend Bob Jakin, Tom raises enough money to pay off his father's debts. Meanwhile, Maggie, who is a clever, emotional girl, and temperamentally the opposite of prosaic, authoritarian, self-controlled Tom, suffers from the deprivation of any intellectual or aesthetic satisfaction and above all from the absence of the love her nature craves. Only her father admires her and he has become increasingly morose, while Tom to whom she has always been devoted is irritated by what he sees as her emotional instability and waywardness. He dislikes the religious fervour of her adolescence and is further antagonised when he discovers her friendship with the crippled Philip Wakem, whose lawyer father is regarded as having engineered Mr Tulliver's downfall. Tom immediately ends this relationship by threatening to tell their father, but very soon after, just when Tom has been able to pay off the creditors, Mr Tulliver dies of a stroke after attacking his enemy, Wakem. Two years later Maggie returns from earning her living in a boarding school to visit her cousin Lucy Deane who is virtually engaged to the wealthy Stephen Guest. Maggie meets Philip again, who wants to marry her, but she and Stephen fall violently in love and partly by chance, they become compromised. Lucy is heartbroken,

Tom furiously angry and St Ogg's full of sanctimonious condemnation of Maggie. A sudden flood sweeps down on the town: Maggie sets off to rescue Tom from the Mill, does so, but then they are both drowned. The book ends with the suggestion that Stephen and Lucy eventually marry.

3.2 CHAPTER SUMMARIES AND CRITICAL COMMENTARY

BOOK 1 BOY AND GIRL

Chapter 1 - Outside Dorlcote Mill

Summary

Most of this first chapter is like a great landscape painting. The eye first rests on the far distance where the Floss crosses a great plain before meeting the sea, noticing the trading ships and the rich farmlands, before moving to the ancient little town of St Ogg's where the Floss is joined by the tributary Ripple. It is from a bridge here that the viewpoint is established, and immediately in front is Dorlcote Mill with its sheltered old house and trees. The third paragraph brings the picture alive with the booming noise of the water-wheel, the thunder of the wagon wheels and the effort of the great dray-horses. Finally the focus closes in on the 'unresting wheel' of the mill itself, a white dog, and a little girl who watches it entranced. These are the foreground figures and because the February afternoon is getting dark, it is time that the little girl went in to the warm glow from the house.

Commentary

This setting of the novel is presented by Eliot as a dream of 'many years ago', as she says in the final paragraph with curiously involuted phraseology. She actually says she had been going to tell the reader about Mr and Mrs Tulliver when she had fallen asleep and dreamt of the Floss and the Mill and Maggie. So the suggestion is that the telling of this novel comes both from her conscious intention and from the strong impulse of a remembered, visionary past. This certainly confirms the idea that the novel is a conscious reworking of some of the elements of her own childhood. This is supported by the insistent juxtaposition of then and now, there and here, the 'little girl' and the speaker so that the reader enters in to the writer's 'dream' of the past. Maggie is gazing at the water-wheel with its endless hypnotic motion, an image of timelessness, but the whole passage is full of water images - sea, tide, wavelets, damp, ducks, pond and so on - and the perceptive reader will notice the link between this first sentence and the famous final one in Book 7.

Book 1, Chapter 2 – Mr Tulliver of Dorlcote Mill, declares his resolution about Tom

Summary

Mr Tulliver tells his wife he is determined to educate their son Tom well, so he can hold his own with people like lawyers, who have made the uneducated Tulliver feel at a disadvantage. He decides to consult the auctioneer and valuer, Riley, about finding a better school than the Academy Tom now attends. As usual, Mrs Tulliver is at cross purposes with her husband, worrying who will do Tom's laundry if he is at a distant school and whether he will have enough to eat. She wants this important decision to be submitted to the consideration of a family council – her three sisters and their husbands, but Mr Tulliver angrily rejects such consultation. His main worry is that Tom, who takes after his mother, is not 'smart' enough to benefit from such education, unlike his nine-year-old sister Maggie. Mrs Tulliver in return points out Maggie's shortcomings – her tomboy qualities, rebelliousness, unmanageable hair, brown skin, dreaminess and hatred of needlework. Maggie herself comes in at this moment and exemplifies all her mother's complaints, but Mr Tulliver only laughs affectionately at his unconventional daughter.

Commentary

The reader has been drawn in to the bright fire in the pleasant house, but finds at once there is no real harmony indoors. Mr Tulliver is uneasily aware of his poor education and jealous of his water-rights; Mrs Tulliver is 'dull-witted' and disappointed that her only daughter in no way resembles the conventional ideal of the period, like her cousin Lucy, while Maggie is irritated by her mother's nagging. All kinds of themes are presented: the chancy nature of heredity, the different educational opportunities of boys and girls, the doubt whether nurture can alter nature, and Mr Tulliver foresees that society will not value a clever woman – 'an over 'cute woman's no better nor a long tailed sheep'. Mrs Tulliver twice gives voice to her fear of Maggie drowning – a premonitory motif that will recur frequently.

Character emerges from dialogue, as in a play, and the use of present tense following the phrase 'Exit Maggie . . . ' illustrates the dramatic concept of the scene. When there is explicit comment it enlarges the reader's awareness from this little domestic scene to, for instance, the cyclical nature of historical change, as in the remark about Mrs Tulliver's cap, or to the contrast between the ideal and the real, as in the reference to Raphael's Madonna, or by means of Mrs Tulliver's pride in her best Holland sheets, to the ludicrous dissonance between human concerns and the inevitability of death.

The integration of characterisation, plot, themes and symbols is shot through with an irrepressible sense of comedy, illustrated here by Mrs Tulliver's extraordinary lateral thinking about moles and shirt-fronts, by Maggie's succinct description of the art of patchwork or by the rueful phraseology of 'small mistake of nature'; the realism of country speech is caught by a limited use of dialectal words like 'franzy', a tactful suggestion of sound in words like 'calkilate' or 'vallyin' and specially in the turn of phrase, as when Tulliver hopes Tom will learn 'a good lot o' words as don't mean much, so as you can't lay hold of 'em i' law'.

Book 1, Chapter 3 – Mr Riley gives his advice concerning a school for Tom

Summary

When Riley calls at Dorlcote Mill the following day, Tulliver asks his advice about Tom's schooling and reveals a further reason for educating his son beyond a miller's needs: he dislikes the idea of Tom impatient to take over the mill before his father wants to retire. The listening Maggie springs to Tom's defence, to her father's fond amusement, and he boasts to Riley of her cleverness and ease in reading. Delighted with their attention, Maggie discourses on the devil in Defoe and Bunyan with such gusto that both are shocked and Maggie's pride is hurt. Meanwhile Riley suggests that Tom goes to board with the Reverend Walter Stelling at King's Norton. Tulliver is dubious about a clergyman's teaching since he wants Tom to become an astute man of business and a parson might be too 'high-learnt' but Riley persuades him Stelling can educate Tom in any style his father wants. Tulliver finally agrees to approach Stelling, though he is taken aback at the high cost: a hundred pounds a year. (Remember, Tom will only earn one pound a week when he starts work: £100 then would be nearer £3000 now.) The chapter ends with an analysis of why Riley has urged Tulliver so strongly to do this.

Commentary

Why does Riley recommend Stelling? The cost is much too high for Tulliver (whose mill is already mortgaged) and the education (as he hazily suspects) will be totally unsuitable. Riley hardly knows the man, only knows his wife by sight and though her father, Mr Timpson, is a business associate, Riley certainly expects no 'definite advantage'. Eliot is fascinated by people's motivation and the concluding four paragraphs map out just how complex are Riley's conscious reasons as well as the 'dim ideas and complacencies' which add extra urgency to his suggestion. Typically, the reader is involved in the moral issues underlying Riley's advice, and this is signalled by the 'we' and the reference to 'our neighbours'. Eliot links the irrationality of the human machine with nature in its wider aspects both in the seed-corn image and the parasite reference of the final paragraph. Tulliver has equally irrational grounds for thinking so highly of Riley's acumen - his 'oracular face' and habit of taking snuff - in fact, far from being canny, he is financially inept as Tulliver finds to his cost when he dies (Book 3, Chapter 1). The theme of a society inimical to women appears again: daughters are a financial burden to Riley (and to Mr Timpson, we gather), Riley's attitude to Maggie - 'silly and of no consequence' - illustrates her father's fear that clever girls are unwelcome, and we hear just why Mr Tulliver chose his wife: 'I picked her from her sisters o' purpose 'cause she was a bit weak-like - for I wasn't a-goin' to be told the rights of things by my own fireside.' It is hardly surprising that for both of them marriage has not been entirely satisfactory. An even harsher note concerning women appears in the picture that Eliot selects for Maggie to explain to Riley. It is the drowning of that scapegoat of society, a witch. 'She's innocent and not a witch,' says Maggie, 'but only a poor silly old woman. But what good would it do her then, you know, when she was drowned?' - a question many readers echo at the end of the novel.

Book 1, Chapter 4 - Tom is expected

Summary

Mrs Tulliver will not let Maggie go with her father to collect Tom from school because the rain might spoil her bonnet. In fury, she wets her hair so her mother cannot curl it and escapes to the attic where she expends her anger upon a wooden doll. However, she cheers up when the sun comes out, and finds Luke, the head miller, to chat to as he works in the mill. She tries to impress him with her learning and is happy until Luke reminds her of the rabbits she had promised to look after while Tom was away: she had forgotten to feed them and they are dead. Maggie is so upset that Luke takes her with him to his cottage to be comforted by his wife. She looks at their series of prints of The Prodigal Son, though Luke refuses to acquiesce in Maggie's hopeful view of his future - Luke thinks he'd never be much use.

Commentary

Maggie is shown here again at odds with her society - battles about her hair are often used as an image of her rebellion against conventional restraints, and we note that Aunt Glegg is invoked as representative of the censorious world. The violence of Maggie's reaction is shown by her violence to her doll and the use of the word 'fetish' suggests the primitive quality of her emotions. But Maggie's nature is as mercurial as it is passionate, and we learn a lot about her in this chapter. She lives a rich imaginative life – 'the spiders were especially a subject of speculation with her' – and feels great kinship with the Prodigal Son since 'he was sorry . . . and wouldn't do wrong again'. She hungers for approval and admiration, but the death of Tom's rabbits indicates a dangerous gulf between her intentions and her actions: the reader is being educated to understand why Tom will so often be angry with her.

The reference to the Prodigal Son, with the problem of whether people do ever change their natures is introduced at the end of the chapter with a deceptively casual air – will Maggie or Tom ever really change?

Book 1, Chapter 5 – Tom comes home

Summary

Tom arrives home from school and tells Maggie he has bought fishing lines so they can go fishing together. But Maggie has to confess that her neglect has killed his rabbits and he abandons her angrily. She retires to her refuge in the attic, determined to stay there until Tom is sorry for his unkindness, but very soon is overwhelmed by her keen desire to be forgiven and to be loved. By this time Tom has got over his anger and his parents send him to fetch Maggie downstairs. She is so glad to see him that he becomes kind and they are reconciled. The next day Tom takes her fishing and by luck she has a catch and they both have a day of idyllic happiness.

Commentary

Maggie's strongest need is to be loved, but it is her tragedy that she nearly always does what will most irritate her idol, Tom. His version of how to love is quite different: to look after, to use, and to punish when necessary, but it is important to notice that there are 'tender fibres' in Tom that will respond to love. When they are happy, both children think of life as essentially unchanging, and in one sense they are right, since the imprint of such early experience is indelible. Eliot's sonnet sequence *Brother and Sister* shows how closely this episode was related to her own experience (see section 1.2). The reference to *Pilgrim's Progress* near the end of the chapter ties together a knot of associations for the reader. These include the raising of the Floss into majestic religious symbolism, Maggie's vision of the world always in terms of her childhood associations, and her imaginative assimilation of what she reads into her own emotional life.

The author's voice comes through often in this near-autobiographical chapter where even the 'wonderful' Round Pool can be traced back to her own childhood at Griff House. There is, first, the chillingly objective prophecy of the difference between Tom's 'indeterminate' ordinary appearance and his actual 'real, inflexible purposes' and a comment on the way the apparent conformity of boys and rebelliousness of girls is often misleading. Then there is the sad comment on 'the bitter sorrows of childhood' followed a few pages later by a comparison of the stiff 'dignified alienation' of adults who have quarrelled, with the animal-like impulsiveness with which Tom and Maggie make friends again. The reiterated use of 'we' (it starts three consecutive sentences) makes this more than the author's individual comment, since it evokes the experience of the reader as well, and this recurs with increased emotional intensity in the last paragraph but one, where the writer's own childhood seems to be used as a pattern for all 'our' childhoods. Even more emphatic is the last paragraph where Eliot speaks directly in the first person and with the present tense: 'The wood I walk in on this mild May morning' to make the reader share her profound conviction that the memories of a childhood world are 'the mother tongue of our imagination'.

So this chapter reflects some of the ways in which she enlarges the novel form. As the critic W. J. Harvey says, she is 'unwilling that the reader should stand outside the fictional world she has so carefully left open and uninsulated' but challenges him 'to bring this fictional world into . . . his own deepest sense of the real world in which he lives'.

Book 1, Chapter 6 – The aunts and uncles are coming

Summary

This chapter preludes the entrance of the formidable Dodson clan, Mrs Tulliver's three sisters and their husbands, and in the conversation between the Tullivers about the forthcoming visit it becomes clear that Mrs Tulliver is aware of the need to ensure her children's possible inheritances from their childless aunts, specially as there will be no such hope from Mr Tulliver's relations. She is sadly aware that Tom dislikes his aunts and Maggie is particularly at disadvantage compared with her well-behaved cousin, Lucy. Meanwhile we see more of Tom and Maggie: there is a revealing incident when they are given some jam puffs to bribe them away from the busy kitchen. Tom insists on a just division, while Maggie only wants Tom to have the larger share. But when she happens to choose the better piece, he accuses her of greed and goes off in dudgeon to play with Bob Jakin, a poor boy who sometimes works for Mr Tulliver as a bird scarer but is highly knowledgeable about animals and indifferent to creature comforts. They toss for Bob's halfpenny: he cannot bear the thought of losing it so cheats, much to Tom's indignation. They fight and with the help of Yap, the dog, Tom wins. He calls Bob a cheat, says he won't have anything more to do with him and returns home.

Commentary

The complex subject of family likeness is explored in connection with the

Dodsons. What makes their particularity? It is their conviction that their way of doing things is the right one, whether preserving gooseberries or arranging funerals. Tom dislikes his aunts but, as his mother knows, he takes after her side of the family. In the Dodson fashion he is 'troubled with no doubts' that everything he does is right, and the two incidents in the second half of the chapter illustrate just this. Both in the case of Maggie and Bob, Tom is convinced his judgement is right and it is his duty to punish offenders against that judgement. Maggie is as insecure as Tom is inexorable - she always wishes 'she had done something different' and her only comfort is to take refuge in fantasies in which she imagines the world as she'd like it to be, a form of self-deception not unlike her father's, and one which Eliot describes as 'her opium'.

Book 1, Chapter 7 - Enter the aunts and uncles

Summary

The three Dodson sisters and their husbands arrive for dinner with the Tullivers. Aunt Glegg shows herself as censorious and thrifty, Aunt Pullet as sentimental, hypochondriac and fond of dress. The Deanes are the most financially successful of the three visiting couples - he is partner in a 'mill-owning, ship-owning business' - and they are the only ones with a child, Lucy, whose fair prettiness contrasts with Maggie's tousled appearance. This draws the criticism of the adults and in desperation Maggie persuades Tom to come upstairs and cut her hair off. But now she looks so odd that Tom laughs at her and Maggie, heartbroken, realises she has done the wrong thing yet again. When she finally creeps downstairs, the family greet her with laughter, horror and reproof, and only her father takes her part. When the three children have gone into the garden, Mrs Tulliver pushes her husband into announcing his plan to send Tom to school with 'a parson'. All are astonished, specially at the idea of such large expenditure for such an uncertain return as education. The three uncles take a neutral stance and so does Aunt Deane - Aunt Pullet tries to keep the peace but battle royal develops between Mr Tulliver and Aunt Glegg. She disapproves of educating Tom above his station, reminds Mr Tulliver that he already owes her money and foresees the family going 'headlongs to ruin'. Mr Tulliver reacts furiously, and unwisely tells his sister-in-law that women should know their place and she is a 'damned ill-tempered woman'. Aunt Glegg leaves in fury, followed by a sad Mr Glegg.

Commentary

Family gatherings are notorious for bringing hidden resentments out into the open. This disastrous party presents a revelation of family characteristics and discords, particularly the Dodson suspicion of Tulliver's 'contrairy' nature, his borrowings and his fondness for lawsuits, as well as the discord between the sisters themselves, their feeling that Mrs Tulliver has married beneath her, and that Maggie will come to no good. Secondly, the gathering evokes in miniature the kind of society that Tom and Maggie will grow up into: the rigidity of its conventions (education, class, dress and mourning are all touched on), the parochialism of the Pullets, the censorious bitterness of Aunt Glegg, the awareness of money and possessions as of prime importance, and the necessity of preserving respectability. The narrative presents two themes, unobtrusively balanced and both providing comic bombshells: Maggie's shorn appearance at the dinner table illustrates her rebellion against convention and her disastrous impulsiveness. She acts violently and then suffers miserably. Similarly Mr Tulliver's announcement of Tom's schooling is equally shocking to his hearers and may be equally disastrous as Uncle Glegg's ominous couplet suggests. Tulliver, like Maggie, is both obstinate and rash.

The episode also demonstrates Eliot's comedy, specially in the sense of the hilarious combination of opposites: Aunt Pullet's care that her tears will not spot her bonnet-strings – Aunt Glegg's use of false curls as a barometer of social occasions; the reasons for Mr Deane's poor opinion of the Prussians. Typical of her style too is the passage on the intensity of childhood grief and the way in which the reader's own experience is evoked.

Lucy makes her first appearance here, and there is the first mention of lawyer Wakem's son, Philip.

Eliot was surprised that the critical reaction to the aunts was largely one of dislike: she had modelled them on her mother's sisters and thought their impact would be predominantly comic. It is interesting to consider why in this case she was mistaken – the reader has already been drawn into sympathy with the children, and though we see Aunt Glegg as comic through adult eyes, we also share the vulnerability and unease of Tom and Maggie as 'she took their hands, hurting them with her large rings'. Perhaps, too, many readers would share Mr Tulliver's dislike of interfering relations.

Book 1, Chapter 8 – Mr Tulliver shows his weaker side

Summary

Mrs Tulliver is worried that her sister Glegg might want her £500 repaid after this quarrel, and with her usual tactlessness asks her husband how he could raise it. Nettled, he decides to repay the debt at once and so rides over the next day to visit his sister and her husband who owe him £300. Mr Moss is a poor, unsuccessful farmer, and they have eight children. When Tulliver asks for repayment, Moss says he'll have to sell up everything to raise the money. Mr Tulliver tries to be firm in his decision but he has always been very fond of his sister, Gritty, and is touched by her fondness for Maggie. He imagines how helpless Maggie might be if Tom were 'hard on her' in the future. After much indecision, he rides back to the Moss's farm and tells his sister he will raise the money in some other way.

Commentary
It emerges that Dorlcote Mill and the house are mortgaged for £2000, though Mrs Tulliver has been kept in ignorance of this, and the reader begins to realise how often money is being mentioned in this novel. Once again the economic burden of girls is stressed - Tulliver foresees that the four little Moss girls may be a burden on their brothers as Gritty has been on him, 'creating a necessity for mortgages', specially when they may produce so many children.

Mr Tulliver changes his mind completely within this episode. First he persuades himself that it will do Moss good to have to raise the money and then, with equal irrationality, that his leniency may in some providential way be of use to Maggie. This 'eddying' of a character's emotions will be seen often in Maggie.

Book 1, Chapter 9 - To Garum Firs

Summary
While Mr Tulliver is visiting the Moss family, Mrs Tulliver, Tom, Maggie, and Lucy go on their promised afternoon visit to Garum Firs, the trim house of the Pullets. Maggie has had a miserable morning because of the hairdresser's disapproval of her mangled hair and because Tom has preferred the docile, neat Lucy as a playmate. Aunt Pullet's house is the quintessence of order, the floors brilliantly polished, furniture shrouded in covers and clothes such as her new bonnet kept in layers of paper and under lock and key. Both Tom and Maggie feel ill at ease there but it is Maggie who drops cake and spills wine, so the children are finally sent out into the garden while Mrs Tulliver asks her sister to help heal the quarrel with Aunt Glegg. Mrs Pullet promises to go and see her the next day.

Commentary
Both Tullivers are trying to do the same thing - that is, solve a money problem, but as usual neither knows what the other is doing and neither will be successful. Mrs Tulliver's worries are contrasted with the prosperity of Garum Firs and the obliging Mr Pullet, with his admiration of his wife's illnesses, is very different from the awkward Tulliver. The chapter holds one of the few occasions when Mrs Tulliver is allowed to have her say and her credo of hard work and superb housekeeping appears in the paragraph ending, 'A woman can do no more nor she can'. That this is not enough is suggested by the melancholy Mrs Pullet's reply, with its prophetic mention

of the sale of all Mrs Tulliver's treasures - but, as she says, 'But what can I do, sister?'

In Eliot's novels the reader is often made to realise that to some problems there is no answer.

Book 1, Chapter 10 - Maggie behaves worse than she expected

Summary

Out in the Pullets' garden Tom has devoted all his attention to Lucy so that Maggie, consumed with jealousy, finally pushes her immaculate cousin into the mud and runs away. The adults are horrified; Mrs Tulliver first wonders if Maggie is drowned and then takes Tom and Lucy back to Dorlcote Mill in case Maggie has fled home.

Commentary

The discord between Maggie and her society is given another dimension here by showing her reaction to Lucy, whose submissive prettiness obviously fulfils Tom's idea of what a girl should be. This rouses in Maggie a jealousy of primitive violence - twice she is compared to Medusa - that recalls her revenge on her wooden doll. Several turns of phrase establish that Maggie's 'fierce thrust' pushes Lucy into something worse than mud, even though Lucy is quite innocent - indeed she likes and admires Maggie. The situation, in fact, is a miniature of Book 7. The water/drowning motif recurs but is given an extra significance by Mrs Pullet's gloomy prognostication that there might be even worse ends for Maggie than drowning.

Book 1, Chapter 11 - Maggie tries to run away from her shadow

Summary

Maggie has, in fact, decided to run away and join the gypsies, hoping they will recognise her talents and give her the admiration she longs for. She finds an encampment on Dunlow Common but the gypsies prove as alien to her as her own family and more frightening. She is greatly relieved when one takes her homewards and they meet Mr Tulliver who comforts her and makes her promise never to run 'away from father' again.

Commentary

Maggie's plan to become 'Queen of the Gypsies' and teach them about Columbus and the use of a wash-basin is in grotesque contrast with the rough reality of dirt, theft and poverty. The episode exemplifies what Eliot says about Maggie's odd 'mixture of clear-eyed acumen and blind dreams', and also the way her reading transforms reality into images of terror with Apollyon, dwarfs and witches. As often, Tom's opinion (in this case of the gypsies) proves essentially accurate, and Maggie learns to regret her precipitancy bitterly.

Maggie's feelings on this expedition are vividly conveyed since the writer moves easily between narration and comment, and a very intimate kind of unspoken soliloquy, so that we are aware of each fleeting thought as it crosses the child's mind.

Book 1, Chapter 12 - Mr and Mrs Glegg at home

Summary

The history, economics and legend of St Ogg's are reviewed before we see the Gleggs in their 'excellent house' at its centre and find Mrs Glegg at odds with her good-tempered husband. He has tried to pacify her after the quarrel of Chapter 7, pointing out the foolishness of calling in her money before she knows of an equally lucrative investment. But she becomes increasingly acrimonious, finally withdrawing upstairs with the air of a martyr. Mr Glegg calms himself by energetic gardening, and Mrs Glegg by the hint her husband has given during their quarrel, that his will has left her well provided. So she decides to let Tulliver keep the money, specially as the interest is good.

Commentary

The changing fortunes of St Ogg's from Roman times to the time of the novel and to the 'present' (notice the shop-windows reference) act as a long perspective against which the fierce breakfast-table hostilities of the Gleggs assume their proper proportion. They are shown as typical products of their society, small-minded, indifferent to history, to religious enthusiasm and to politics, intent on their own small 'slow gains' and unquestioning of the St Ogg's system of values. But they are brought to vivid life by the spirited illogic of their quarrel and by the different manifestations in them of the same spirit of thrift. We learn that Mr Glegg 'chose' his wife because of her thrift, but like Mr Tulliver (Book 1, Chapter 3), finds disadvantages in this approach to matrimony. The legend of St Ogg's is given in detail. Maggie will dream about it at the climax of the book (Book 6, Chapter 14) and the setting of river and storm anticipates the final flood so it must be considered significant. The moral seems to be that the most crucial duty is that of active compassion, a compassion that will continue beyond the bounds of reason. There is an ironic twist in putting this little story in the same chapter as the prudent Gleggs.

Book 1, Chapter 13 – Mr Tulliver further entangles the skein of life

Summary
Mrs Pullet carries out her promise to her sister by visiting Mrs Glegg to make peace and finds her willing to continue her loan to the Tullivers. But Mrs Tulliver tells her husband of her intervention on his behalf and, infuriated, he immediately writes off to cancel the agreement. To raise the £500, he then has to borrow through the man he most distrusts, the lawyer Wakem. Relations between Tulliver and Aunt Glegg remain strained and Tom goes off to his new school.

Commentary
Money concerns govern this chapter, too, but there is a contrast between Mrs Glegg whose sense of family duty would never let her alter her will simply out of dislike for her brother-in-law, and Tulliver, whose money dealings here are certainly not governed by consideration for his family. The reference to Oedipus makes the ironic point that Mr Tulliver's concerns are of as great significance to him as were those of the famous tragic hero, but debatable since it is Tulliver's unfortunate temperament, not 'external fact' which is driving him into ever deeper financial waters. Tom's departure for an expensive school implicitly predicts yet more money troubles.

BOOK 2 SCHOOL TIME

Chapter 1 – Tom's 'first half'

Summary
Tom is unhappy at school. The Reverend Walter Stelling is a genial man but his educational methods are unimaginatively traditional, and Tom is totally at sea with Latin and geometry since he cannot connect these with any of the realities he knows. His self-confidence is sapped by realising that his speech and manners are unacceptable, and his physical abilities count for nothing. Being the only pupil, he is very lonely, missing Maggie and even enjoys playing with the two-year-old Laura. Maggie's arrival on a fortnight's visit is very welcome: she enjoys encountering Latin and Euclid and is a great success with Mr Stelling. When she enquires whether she could study like Tom, however, Stelling gives his verdict that girls are 'quick and shallow'.

Commentary
Maggie's intellectual curiosity and ability are in strong contrast with Tom's deficiency here: the irony of her exclusion from academic study is self-evident. Tom's education is obviously not going to be the kind that his father hopes. The final paragraph is not only about Tom's profound emotional attachment to the familiar things of home: Eliot uses first person pronouns to draw the reader in to a sympathetic sharing of experience.

Eliot's method of projecting characters is exemplified even in this brief portrait of the Stellings – the use of significant physical particulars, of ironic, mock-innocent detail (about sermons, for instance), the startling contrast between a self-image and other viewpoints, and also a typical reminder that any character may surprise us. Though his fellow clerics think Mr Stelling 'a dull dog', yet he will be shown acting 'wisely' in the next chapter, and even the self-centred Mrs Stelling later shows a kindness in Chapter 7 which touches Maggie deeply.

Book 2, Chapter 2 – The Christmas holidays

Summary
Seasonal Christmas festivities at Dorlcote Mill include a family dinner with all the Moss family. Mr Tulliver talks of his determination to stop a new neighbour, Pivart, from irrigating his land and thus reducing the mill's water-supply. Mrs Moss and Mrs Tulliver fear he will once again go to law: but the latter's repeated appeals to keep clear of lawsuits only strengthen his determination to do so, a determination further increased by his enmity for Pivart's lawyer, Wakem. Tom's holiday is marred by his father's increasing irritability over these matters, and by learning that Wakem's crippled son Philip will be joining him at Mr Stelling's next term.

Commentary
The troubles of the adult world begin to break in on Tom as he notices, but does not understand, the change in his father, whose obstinacy is made worse by his wife's tactlessness. The loveliness of the natural world under snow and the Christmas rituals are an ironic background to the frictions within the Mill.

Book 2, Chapter 3 – The new schoolfellow

Summary
On Tom's return to school he meets Philip, an intelligent, sensitive, fifteen-year-old with a gift for drawing. Tom admires his abilities but suspects him because he is Wakem's son and because he is 'a hunchback'. Philip sees

Tom as a 'well-made barbarian' and feels some bitterness at the contrast between them.

Commentary

There is a typical 'eddying of feeling' in Tom's reaction to Philip which will recur while they are together at school, but his inability to adjust to new ideas means he can never fully dissociate Philip from his unscrupulous father or from his ideas about cripples. His natural inclination to make rigid judgements is just that quality that Eliot most deplores (see section 4.2).

Book 2, Chapter 4 – 'The young idea'

Summary

Tom finds Philip's stories of battles and heroes fascinating and is grateful for help with his Latin, but Philip's deformity has made him over-sensitive to Tom's tactless patronage and they have stormy quarrels. Tom borrows a sword from his drillmaster, a Peninsular War veteran: he intends to astonish Maggie with it on her next visit.

Commentary

Tom's initial shock of fright at the sword exercise (though he refuses to admit this) is what precipitates a bitter quarrel with Philip and startles Tom into betraying his deepest convictions: 'Your father's a rogue and you're no better than a girl'. Tom's fixity of impression and Philip's vulnerability are demonstrated here. Boys' education at this time is shown as a hit-or-miss affair. Both private tuition and grammar schools were usually inadequate for their middle-class clientele because of their outmoded curricula and methods, often coupled (though not here) with inefficiency and laziness. So Tom really suffers as much as Maggie from a hide-bound and uncongenial system.

Book 2, Chapter 5 – Maggie's second visit

Summary

When Maggie arrives, Philip and Tom are still hostile. Maggie watches them at their lessons and is attracted to Philip, partly because he is deformed, as well as being so clever. Philip thinks it would be nice to have a sister like her. After Tom has done his prep. he takes Maggie upstairs, makes her hide her eyes and appears dressed up like a pirate, complete with burnt-cork eyebrows and Poulter's sword. He then terrifies her, by attempting the sword exercise, but the sword is too heavy for him and drops on his foot: Tom faints.

Commentary
Tom needs this display to balance his academic inferiority, but the accident reflects his lack of judgement and may suggest how unprepared he is for a real sword – that is, real trouble. It is typical that he seems to have no imagination of how frightened Maggie will be, and this kind of obtuseness will cause her much misery later on. Their difference is further shown in her attitude to deformity, which is exactly the opposite to Tom's.

Book 2, Chapter 6 – A love scene

Summary
Mr Askern, the surgeon, dresses Tom's wound, but only Philip realises that Tom's main worry is whether he will be lame. He finds out all will be well, carries the reassuring news to Tom, and old enmities are momentarily forgotten. Maggie sees a lot of Philip and wishes he was another brother. After Maggie's departure, however, the boys' relationship sinks back into intermittent antipathy.

Commentary
Tom's accident provides the opportunity for Philip and Maggie to establish an affectionate relationship which will be of great importance later in the novel. Maggie's instinctive affection is contrasted with Tom's innate suspicion of anything different – in this he is like his father whose remarks about Philip's heredity carry ironic overtones to the reader. Maggie's fondness for deformed things is linked with her 'unsatisfied, beseeching affection' and she realises sadly how Tom's affection is not, like her's, boundless. The brief mention of Yap's illness is a sad note suggesting childhood is nearly over.

Book 2, Chapter 7 – The Golden Gates are passed

Summary
Tom is sixteen and in his final term at school and Maggie, now thirteen, is, we hear, at boarding school with Lucy. One morning Maggie appears suddenly at King's Norton with the news that their father has lost the lawsuit, is financially ruined and has had a stroke. Tom immediately leaves school and returns home with Maggie.

Commentary
This triple blow is the end of childhood, and is rendered more traumatic by Tom's total unpreparedness for the disaster and because bankruptcy in the St Ogg's world carries a stigma of disgrace that Tom cannot bring himself to associate with his family.

BOOK 3 THE DOWNFALL

Chapter 1 – What had happened at home

Summary
When Mr Tulliver had first heard the lawsuit was lost, he seemed to persuade himself he could ride out the storm by borrowing from the Pullets and becoming a tenant of Furley, who now holds the mortgage on the mill. The discovery that this mortgage has been transferred to Wakem precipitates a stroke. He has already sent a note to Maggie's school summoning her home, and he recognises her briefly, but his memory has gone. The aunts come and see their prognosis of ruin has been fulfilled and Maggie decides to fetch Tom home immediately.

Commentary
Eliot analyses the reaction of a proud, obstinate man to disaster: first the self-delusion, the conviction that things can be favourably arranged and then the overwhelming shock of reality. She points out the material of tragedy here, no less important because it is set in common life. This idea she extends to make her readers recognise the frequent blighting effect of disasters, similar to those of Mr Tulliver, on whole families, and finally enlarges the reference by a comparison with the animal world. At least two elements prevent simplification here. Mr Tulliver's ruin does not only derive from his litigiousness: a kindly loan to Riley the auctioneer has cost him £250. Further, Mr Tulliver sends for Maggie before he has heard of the transfer of the mortgage to Wakem: there is one part of him which knows he is fooling himself (see also section 5.3).

Book 3, Chapter 2 – Mrs Tulliver's teraphim, or household gods

Summary
Tom and Maggie arrive home to find a bailiff in the house and Mrs Tulliver weeping in deep distress over her household treasures – tablecloths she had spun and marked herself, china and silver she had saved for when she was a girl. Tom for the first time thinks of his father with reproach, and comforts his mother with promises of his support. Their mutual sympathy irritates Maggie who reproaches them violently for blaming her father and thinking of material things. Tom's indignation with Maggie is lessened when he joins her beside Mr Tulliver's sick bed, where he lies helpless.

Commentary
This is Mrs Tulliver's chapter: in her own idiom she recalls her girlhood as she mourns these treasured possessions. Her fear of beggary and the work-

house, the sharp contrast between past and present, the injury she feels done to her children move the reader as well as Tom. Her innocent delight in her gold-sprigged china is in strong contrast with the 'coarse dingy man' smelling of tobacco downstairs and reminds us what she has suffered from the obstinacy and indeed, deceit, of her husband. Tom and Maggie's reactions are typically different, for Tom responds to disaster with an obstinate courage and Maggie is emotionally intemperate.

Book 3, Chapter 3 – The family council

Summary

Gleggs, Pullets and Mrs Deane assemble at Dorlcote Mill to consult. Mrs Tulliver is principally concerned that her 'treasures' will not be auctioned to strangers but is sharply reminded that necessities such as beds and tables come first. The aunts send for the children to impress their dependence upon them. With considerable self-control Tom suggests they prevent the sale and he will pay the interest on their loan. Aunt Glegg angrily dissents and Maggie breaks out in anger against their useless interference. Suddenly Mrs Moss arrives, conscience-stricken because of their £300 debt to Mr Tulliver, but admitting they would have to sell up their farm to repay it. Tom reveals his father once told him never to press the Mosses for this money, and Mr Glegg agrees that in that case they ought to find and destroy the I.O.U. at once.

Commentary

Aunt Glegg appears in a particularly unattractive light. It emerges she had refused to join her sisters in sponsoring Maggie's education, she intervenes to prevent Tom's plan even though she would have had her 5 per cent interest, and her language is bitterly censorious. Her attitude towards her browbeaten sister is in sharp contrast to Mr Tulliver's care for his sister. Tom's financial suggestion and his determination to carry out his father's wishes about her debt shows both sense and integrity while Maggie's outburst, though understandable is, as Tom points out, counter-productive.

Book 3, Chapter 4 – A vanishing gleam

Summary

Tom and Mr Glegg attempt to find Moss's promissory note in Mr Tulliver's oak chest but the noise suddenly rouses the sick man to consciousness. He says the note must be destroyed and asks Tom to see that an investment of £50 from Luke, the head miller, is repaid. Then his lucidity tails away into anger against lawyers and worry about his children's future, and he relapses into unconsciousness, though Mr Turnbull the surgeon is encouraging about his eventual recovery.

Commentary
The most 'prominent ideas' in Mr Tulliver's mind are not his own worries but how to prevent harm to the most vulnerable, like his sister and Luke: in this he and Tom are of one mind.

Book 3, Chapter 5 – Tom applies his knife to the oyster

Summary
Tom, determined to earn money, applies to his Uncle Deane for work at Guest & Co., a general trading firm in St Ogg's in which his uncle has a share. His uncle questions him about his education and Tom is made to realise that he knows nothing useful such as book-keeping. If he is to be successful he will have to start in the warehouse, but no definite job is offered yet. Tom returns dispiritedly to the Mill, and vents some of his disappointment on Maggie whom he rebukes for her outburst the day before.

Commentary
The inanity of Tom's education and that of many others is demonstrated here and contrasted with what the early nineteenth century really needed, that is, some preparation for a world of expanding commerce, technology and science. Tom's experience is shown as embittering and since Maggie depends on Tom for emotional support, she suffers too, and in a way the final paragraph suggests may be disastrous. This paragraph was omitted in the first edition: possibly Eliot at first did not wish to modulate from the emotion of the previous paragraphs to the cool objectivity of historical and scientific comparisons. However, its later reinstatement underlines the way in which Maggie's individual distress must be seen in the wider context of the danger of frustrated powers.

Book 3, Chapter 6 – Tending to refute the popular prejudice against the present of a pocket-knife

Summary
While the contents of their home are being auctioned, the family sit upstairs by the bedside of the unconscious Mr Tulliver. His wife suffers particularly as she imagines her household treasures being dispersed to strangers. When the bidders have gone, Bob Jakin turns up. He wants to give Tom his total wealth – nine sovereigns – which he had intended to use to set up as a pedlar. Tom and Maggie are touched by his generosity

but refuse the money, though Maggie promises they will always call on him for help when they need it.

Commentary
Bob's generosity contrasts strongly with the niggardliness of the aunts and uncles, exemplified by the bareness of the parlour and the disappearance of Maggie's beloved books. His cheerful ability to fend for himself also compares with Tom's difficulty in finding work.

Book 3, Chapter 7 – How a hen takes to stratagem

Summary
Tom is given a temporary job in Guest & Co.'s warehouse and starts evening lessons in book-keeping. Mr Tulliver's assets will not meet his debts, so the Mill must be auctioned. It is possible that Guest & Co. will buy it as an investment and put Tulliver in as manager. Mrs Tulliver decides to assist this by visiting Wakem secretly and asking him not to bid against Guest & Co. Wakem has not previously thought of doing so but at once picks up the idea, decides to buy the Mill himself, and sends his clerk for information about the sale.

Commentary
Mrs Tulliver's interference is as disastrous here as it has always been when she attempted to influence her husband – this is because, in her simplicity, she has no conception of how complicated are most people's motives. This is analysed in regard to Wakem's change of plan. We learn that he thinks of the purchase of the Mill as an excellent investment, and of the 'practical rural kind' he enjoys. He will outwit Guest & Co. of whose influence in the town he is jealous. The Mill will possibly provide for the future of a favourite illegitimate son. Above all, Tulliver will be totally humiliated, but to the onlooker Wakem's action will appear benevolent and disinterested.

Book 3, Chapter 8 – Daylight on the wreck

Summary
Mr Tulliver at last is well enough to come downstairs for the first time since his stroke but only gradually takes in what has happened in the last two months, and that Wakem is now the owner of Dorlcote Mill. He looks at the family bible where his marriage of eighteen years before is recorded and asks his wife not to 'bear him ill-will'. She takes advantage of his unusually humble state and urges him to accept Wakem's offer to employ Tulliver as his manager. Overcome by his feelings of failure, he consents.

Commentary
The reference to Riley's daughters, one of whom had had to become an under-teacher, is relevant to the problem of what Maggie will do in the future. Tulliver's distress about his financial failure is underlined by Luke's sympathy and by Tom's determination to pay off all creditors - but even if he does so his father feels his own life will have been wasted. Eliot's generalisation about the different effects on Tom and Maggie of their father's dependent weakness shows a deference to traditional Victorian views on sexual differences.

Book 3, Chapter 9 - An item added to the family register

Summary
As Tulliver recovers strength, he regrets his promise to work under Wakem but financial stringency and hatred of asking help from the aunts make it inevitable. And as he explains to Luke, he could not bear to leave the Mill where his family have lived for generations. One evening when Tom returns from work, he demands that his son write into the family bible a declaration, explaining why he has accepted service under Wakem and his hope that evil will befall him; Tom also is to sign a promise of lasting enmity. In spite of Maggie's horrified protests, Tom obeys his father's wishes.

Commentary
Tulliver's reasons for staying on are almost as complex as Wakem's in Chapter 7, but the main motivation is the vital link between his life and the Mill. The minutest details of the building are interwoven with memories of his childhood and his parents so that he feels life for him elsewhere would be impossible. In the same way, he is setting his mark upon Tom, by demanding his partnership in this malediction so formally inscribed beside the births and deaths in the bible. Maggie's protest is against what her father is here doing to Tom.

BOOK 4 THE VALLEY OF HUMILIATION

Chapter 1 - A variation of Protestantism unknown to Bossuet

Summary
Eliot turns aside from narrative to discuss the unromantic nature of the subject matter she has chosen. She contrasts two kinds of ruins seen on the banks of the Rhine: the impressive castles and the dismal ruined

villages left behind by floods. Even calamity cannot make the latter impressive, as misfortune will not make 'these emmet-like Dodsons and Tullivers sublime'. Science, however, teaches that every minute part of the living world is equally significant, so to understand what happens to Maggie and Tom we must study the inhibiting conditions each young generation encounters – in this case the deadening effect of unquestioned conventionality, unleavened by any spiritual life. Though St Ogg's consider itself Protestant, it is in fact governed by a blind worship of traditions, some of them good like honesty and hard work and family loyalty, but many mere customs like the proper type of funeral. Though Dodson and Tulliver types differ in detail, neither has any conception of spiritual values. Mr Tulliver, therefore, sees nothing incongruous in his vindictive entry in the family bible.

Commentary
This chapter occurs at the centre of the book and is a typical communiqué from Eliot to her readers, in that it asks an intellectual as well as the emotional response she knows they will have given to the Tulliver disasters. She directs her readers to see her tale in a sociological context, to understand why St Ogg's people are like this. Her own attitude is typically mid nineteenth century, for she thinks in terms of Darwinian science: she assumes an 'onward tendency of human things', a belief in some kind of progress. Her first paragraph with its references to castles and chivalry reflects her awareness of the typical settings of the Romantic Movement as used by the novelist, Sir Walter Scott and the poet, Lord Byron, but she turns away from these to her own quite different style of investigation of 'the mystery of the human lot'.

Book 4, Chapter 2 – The torn nest is pierced by thorns

Summary
Maggie's unhappiness increases as life at the Mill settles into a monotonous and straitened regime. Mrs Tulliver cannot come to terms with her changed world and Mr Tulliver avoids all old acquaintances because he is so ashamed of his debts. Though he wants Maggie near him, the sight of her feeds his bitterness since he fears that poverty will ruin her future and all his energy goes into rigid thrift. Like his father, Tom is single-minded in determination to pay off the debt, and neither of them gives to Maggie any of the tenderness her nature craves.

Commentary
There is no sentimentality here in this review of the long-term effects of poverty and worry. Maggie finds it more difficult to feel tenderness for

her father and Tom sees his parents' shortcomings more clearly. At least Tom and his father have work to do – there seems no useful role in society for Maggie.

Book 4, Chapter 3 – A voice from the past

Summary
Mr Tulliver's temper becomes more savage and Maggie fears what he may do. Bob Jakin turns up with a present of second-hand books for Maggie, and among them she finds a book, *The Imitation of Christ* by Thomas à Kempis, a mediaeval mystic. Its message of selfless renunciation excites her, and over the next two years she attempts to adopt this way of life. She abandons the attempt at self-education from Tom's old school books, tries to learn self-control, and manages to earn some money by doing 'plain sewing' for a local shop, though Tom disapproves of his sister's initiative here. Mrs Tulliver becomes fonder of Maggie as she grows tall and good-looking, but her father's gloom is intensified because his mismanagement has damaged her chances of marrying well.

Commentary
This chapter spans two years and shows one aspect of Maggie's rites of passage into adolescence. Her craving for happiness finds satisfaction in religious enthusiasm but she does not realise that happiness, too, must be renounced. There is an echo here of the period of religious devotion in Eliot's own youth, but Maggie's fervour is linked to her emotional and aesthetic deprivation – she has no music, no art, no books, no loving companionship to feed upon. Bob's admiration and respect for Maggie balance Tom's coldness, and his optimism offsets the dreariness of the Tulliver household. Mumps (like Yap earlier) is important – he emphasises Maggie's forlorn condition.

BOOK 5 WHEAT AND TARES

Chapter 1 – In the Red Deeps

Summary
Walking near her home Maggie, now seventeen, encounters Philip Wakem. He admits he has been trying to meet her since catching a glimpse of her a few days earlier. Though it is five years since they met, Maggie feels a sisterly tenderness for Philip and sadly explains why family enmity precludes another meeting. Philip, who is in love with her, rejects Maggie's ascetic ideas of self-sacrifice, arguing both the need for self-fulfilment and

his own need for her companionship. Maggie is torn between the longing for congenial friendship and fear of deceiving her family, so postpones her decision.

Commentary
Philip, with his talk about pictures, music and books, and above all his devotion, awakens Maggie's repressed natural self. Like Maggie, Eliot had the same experience of trying to finish Scott's *The Pirate* for herself and contemporary readers (for everyone read Scott) would know Minna's love for Cleveland will be frustrated (like Maggie's) and also be aware of the novel's emotive background of wild stormy waters. The setting for this meeting, the time of year, and the name, the Red Deeps, all carry sexual suggestion which explain Eliot's 'uneasiness' in looking at Maggie. In fact it is only Philip who is now in love, but here is another warning of the 'fierce collision' to come as Maggie grows into womanhood.

Book 5, Chapter 2 – Aunt Glegg learns the breadth of Tom's thumb

Summary
Tom has devoted himself single-mindedly to commerce, thereby winning respect from his aunts and uncles. Bob Jakin suggests the possibility of private trading through a friend who travels overseas. Mr Tulliver is reluctant to risk the hard-won savings in such investment, but Tom takes Bob to visit the Gleggs, where he not only demonstrates his salesmanship but helps persuade them to lend Tom some capital. The ventures prosper and Tom hopes to pay off his father's debts by the end of next year, though he keeps this secret.

Commentary
The traditional contrast between the passive role of women and the active one of men is emphasised in the first paragraph. Tom's character sets into saturnine self-reliance which cuts him off emotionally from his family, and this is shown by the ambiguity of his motives for keeping his business success secret. Bob's ability to con Mrs Glegg into buying anything he wishes is a comic variation on the theme of deception and self-deception which has darker overtones with regard to Tom, Maggie, and Philip.

Book 5, Chapter 3 – The wavering balance

Summary
Maggie meets Philip again to say goodbye since she feels the secrecy entailed in their meetings would be wrong. Philip protests against the waste of her natural gifts and warns her that she is deceiving herself with

her narrow concept of self-sacrifice and that such repression carries dangerous consequences. He asks Maggie at least not to forbid him to walk in the Red Deeps so that they may occasionally meet by chance and Maggie's silence consents.

Commentary
As usual, Maggie's prudence is overridden by her emotion. Philip's understanding of her nature is more profound than her own and this enables him to get his way. Maggie wants the calm of a clear conscience but hungers for Philip's companionship. He genuinely thinks her attitude foolish, but speaks so vehemently because of his longing to be with her, a longing intensified by his feeling of being an outsider.

Book 5, Chapter 4 – Another love scene

Summary
Maggie and Philip have been meeting for nearly a year. He has been her 'tutor', supplying books and discussing them. Now he confesses his love for her and beseeches her to tell him if she can love him. Maggie is taken aback but finally says she doesn't think she could love anyone better and that she would like never to part from Philip.

Commentary
The title of the chapter echoes the friendship of their first meeting (Book 2, Chapter 6). The quality of Philip's love has changed since then but the suggestion is that Maggie's is the same affectionate friendship. Eliot's understanding of how speech, as in Maggie's declaration, can be 'at once sincere and deceptive', is typical of her precise moral observation and so is the way Maggie assimilates her affection into religious feeling (last paragraph but one). Philip's remark about Maggie winning lovers away from Lucy and the curious wording of Maggie's response will be remembered later in the book as will the reiterated theme of fair and dark women.

Book 5, Chapter 5 – The cloven tree

Summary
A chance remark by Aunt Pullen that she's always seeing Philip near the Red Deeps, and Maggie's subsequent embarrassment arouse Tom's suspicion of what is happening. He returns home unexpectedly, finds Maggie about to set out to meet Philip, and after making her confess what has happened, he orders her to swear to part with Philip and threatens otherwise to tell their father. Then he takes Maggie with him to confront Philip. There is a violent quarrel, but Philip accepts that Maggie must pro-

tect her father from knowledge of the affair and leaves, assuring her of his constancy. Maggie accuses her brother of moral arrogance and of cruelty since he enjoys punishing her. They part in anger. Maggie finds herself unable to forgive Tom but also relieved at times that she cannot see Philip.

Commentary
The title of the chapter is linked to Philip's fear that the cloven pine is a bad omen (Chapter 4). Not only is Philip and Maggie's relationship split but the crisis has made old resentments boil over so that Maggie and Tom are equally sundered. Again we have to look at motivation - Tom does not realise his, and is incapable of recognising the justice of Maggie's accusations. She too is mistaken about her feelings, as the last sentences and the question at the end suggest.

Book 5, Chapter 6 - The hard-won triumph

Summary
Three weeks later Tom announces to the family that he has made enough money to pay off all the debts. Mr Tulliver is at first speechless, but then overwhelmed with delight and pride in his son and Maggie admires what Tom has achieved. In the night Mrs Tulliver is alarmed by her husband's bad dream in which he seems to be attacking Wakem.

Commentary
This chapter helps restore the balance in regard to Tom. Like Maggie, the reader admires what he has done - he has restored his father's pride even though we know from Chapter 2 how culpable Tom now realises his father to have been. The suddenness of his announcement, however, may not be good for his father, as the dream suggests.

Book 5, Chapter 7 - A day of reckoning

Summary
The next day Mr Tulliver and Tom celebrate the paying of debts by a dinner with creditors. Tulliver seems to have become his old self again but on his way home encounters and attacks Wakem. Maggie, hearing the noise, eventually manages to restrain him. That night Tulliver becomes ill and as he lies dying, tells Tom to try and buy the Mill back and to look after his mother and Maggie. She begs him to forgive Wakem but the old man believes to the end that he has been an honest man, badly treated by the world. His death brings Tom and Maggie together again.

Commentary
Though the abrupt juxtaposition of rejoicing and disaster might at first appear melodramatic, the fuse of this violent episode has been long and carefully laid. Tom should have prepared his father more gradually for the change of fortune; Maggie has feared 'something irretrievably disgraceful' of this nature from years back (Book 4, Chapter 3). Tulliver's 'long-smothered hate' of Wakem has been a theme of the book throughout, signalled again by his dream the night before and by the mounting irritation of his ride home, 'simmering'. Like his daughter, he is incapable of prudence. As usual, the reader sympathises with the stricken Maggie, but the really poignant figure is surely Tom, who earlier that day had 'made the single speech of his life'.

BOOK 6 THE GREAT TEMPTATION

Chapter 1 – A duet in paradise

Summary
Two years have passed. Lucy Deane, whose mother is now dead, is entertaining Stephen Guest one morning: they are not engaged but both envisage this as likely. She tells him her cousin Maggie, who has been away teaching for two years, is coming to stay the next day. Maggie's mother now acts as housekeeper in the pleasant Deane house, and Stephen imagines Maggie will be like her mother. Lucy does not disabuse him, and warns him of the awkwardness between the Tullivers and Philip Wakem, who also visits the Deane house frequently to join in amateur music-making.

Commentary
Lucy has been absent from the story for a long time and Stephen Guest has only been mentioned in rather mocking terms by Mr Deane (Book 3, Chapter 5). Lucy is shown as possessing a rare quality of imaginative kindness in relation to Maggie, to her aunt and, typically, in tenderness to all her pet animals. The presentation of Stephen as idle, self-confident and a shade patronising (illustrated by his choice of duet) caused early reviewers much misgiving. He is in strong contrast with the energetic Tom and the sensitive Philip and a less sympathetic introduction can hardly be imagined.

The implicit luxury of the scene contrasts with the bareness of Maggie's home and the tableau of the opening has an ominous echo of Philip's joking description in Book 5, Chapter 4. The chapter title is ironic since it seems to cast Lucy and Stephen as Adam and Eve, which puts Maggie in the role of the temptress: indeed, Stephen's first reaction to Maggie in the next chapter is 'an alarming amount of devil'.

Book 6, Chapter 2 – First impressions

Summary
Maggie has arrived and her conversation with Lucy sketches in the dreary and restricted life she has been living while helping in a boarding school; Maggie contrasts Lucy's generous delight in others' happiness with her own bitterness. Lucy is confident that she can dispel such gloom with pleasure, specially music and mentions Philip as another part-singer. Before Maggie has time to explain the situation, Stephen appears. He is very struck with Maggie's beauty, intelligence and originality and Maggie is startled by his admiration and finds him both conceited and fascinating. The three go rowing and Stephen teaches Maggie to row. The Pullets call, and plans are made for Maggie to have new clothes.

Commentary
Lucy's emotional reactions in this scene are as straightforward as Stephen and Maggie's are complex. Each feels challenged by the other: Stephen is intrigued by a woman so unlike any he knows, and Maggie's inexperience of the world leaves her vulnerable both to Stephen's masculine appeal and to his desire to impress this unusual woman. His method of doing this – by describing a recent book on the relationship between theology and geology – is of course exactly the right way of rousing Maggie's interest – it recalls the way Philip had wooed her by lending her novels.

The society of St Ogg's gains definition in the conversation: the new vicar, Dr Kenn, who is a selfless high-Anglican, the social importance of the Guest family, and a bazaar for which all the ladies of the district are working.

Book 6, Chapter 3 – Confidential moments

Summary
Lucy comes in to Maggie's bedroom later that night to discover her in a state of emotional excitement after the evening's music with Stephen. Lucy has arranged for Philip to come the next evening so they can sing together. Maggie explains that she must get Tom's permission before she can encounter Philip. Lucy is shocked and Maggie tells her the history of her relationship to Philip. Lucy is fired with romantic determination to make the story end happily.

Commentary
Maggie explains her excitement as the effect of music but the reader is aware from the second and third paragraphs that it is not only the music that has roused her, and her comment to Lucy on the way to treat a lover

is revealing. Eliot points out that Maggie's account of her affair with Philip is sincere yet misleading, since Maggie's understanding of what is happening lags behind her instinctive response - notice her premonitory shiver.

Book 6, Chapter 4 - Brother and sister

Summary
Tom is now lodging with the newly-married Bob Jakin in an old house by the river and it is here that Maggie visits him the next day. Bob is worried about Tom's solitariness and there is a suggestion that Tom may be in love with Lucy. Tom finally agrees to release Maggie from her promise in order to avoid social awkwardness, but his opinion of Maggie's lack of judgement is unchanged and Maggie feels her old resentment against his harshness. But his desire to protect her softens their animosity and they part kindly.

Commentary
The suggestion that Tom is in love with Lucy is explicit here for the first time, though Book 6, Chapter 1 hinted this, typically involving the present of the spaniel: this makes Tom's bitterness more comprehensible. The contrary temperaments of brother and sister are emphatically restated here and contrasted with the links established in their childhood - but the reader recalls vividly how differently they regarded each other even then. The different conventional roles of men and women are underlined: Tom feels Maggie has behaved improperly by establishing her humble economic independence instead of relying on his protection and authority.

Book 6, Chapter 5 - Showing that Tom had opened the oyster

Summary
Tom is now twenty-three and has been working at Guest & Co. for seven years. Mr Deane announces they plan to give him a share in the business since he has done so well, and Tom confides his ambition to regain the Mill, as he had promised his father. Mr Deane promises to consider the firm's acquiring it for Tom to manage and eventually buy.

Commentary
Mr Deane's comments on the increasing tempo of economic and industrial life are exemplified by the likelihood of Tom's achieving success so much younger than his uncle. The ironic remark about Stephen's verbal facility may link with Mr Deane's regret that he has no son like Tom - does he regard this possible son-in-law with mixed feelings? Tom's final remark is a timely reminder of the deprivation he, as well as Maggie, has suffered.

Book 6, Chapter 6 – Illustrating the laws of attraction

Summary
Maggie blossoms in the social attention and admiration of St Ogg's. Philip is away sketching and by his return the relationship between Maggie and Stephen has become electric, though Lucy does not notice this. Maggie is too inexperienced to recognise what is happening, and Stephen refuses to admit the dangers of the situation.

Commentary
The dry scientific tone of the chapter's title underlines the refusal to apportion blame here. Maggie's 'characteristics' are as unalterable as Stephen's or Tom's, but all their histories are unpredictable simply because destiny depends on chance as much as character: Eliot instances how easy would Hamlet's lot have been if his uncle had died young. Incident (Stephen's evening visit), language ('oppressively conscious . . . even to the finger ends') and the reiterated sensuous images ('tiny silken pet', 'long curly ears . . . drooped', 'stroking', 'closely hovering' etc.) make us vividly aware of the sexual attraction between Stephen and Maggie and of their helplessness.

Book 6, Chapter 7 – Philip re-enters

Summary
When Philip reappears one rainy morning he and Maggie swiftly re-establish their old friendship. But Philip senses a change in Maggie and when Stephen arrives and they settle down to a morning's music he chooses a song of forsaken love. Later he notices how eager Stephen is to be near Maggie and he becomes suspicious of the truth. At lunch Mr Deane surprises them by asking Philip about his father's farming interests and Lucy later coaxes her father into telling her of the plan to buy Dorlcote Mill back from Wakem if possible. She is sure she can enlist Philip's support here and thinks Tom's resulting gratitude might win his consent to Maggie and Philip's marriage.

Commentary
Maggie's sudden memory from two years before of Philip's joke about Lucy's lovers (Book 5, Chapter 4) reveals her situation with a sudden unwelcome clarity, but for the reader it intensifies the feeling of Maggie's helplessness in the face of her own nature and chance. For the way music is utilised in this scene see section 5.6.

Book 6, Chapter 8 – Wakem in a new light

Summary
Philip invites his father to look at his new sketches among which he has placed two of Maggie. Wakem is at first angry to hear of his son's love for a member of a family he detests but is influenced by memory of his beloved dead wife not to stand in the way of Philip achieving similar happiness if this proves possible. So he agrees to let Philip tell Deane that he will sell Dorlcote Mill back to Tom.

Commentary
This is the only time we see Philip alone with his father and the complex uneasy relationship between them recalls that between Tom and his father. Wakem's tenderness for Philip prevents the reader seeing him solely as the cunning villain of Tulliver's imagination. The economic basis of this society shows through again: Philip and the possibility of his marrying are totally dependent on his father who here pronounces the bleakest view of the position of women in the whole novel: 'We don't ask what a woman does – we ask whom she belongs to.' Philip's dream is yet another premonition of the climax of the novel.

Book 6, Chapter 9 – Charity in full dress

Summary
Maggie's stall at the Charity Bazaar is successful and her appearance much admired. Mr Wakem is a customer and takes pains to be pleasant. At first Stephen keeps near Lucy but finally surrenders to his longing to speak with Maggie; she, however, is miserably conscious of Philip's awareness and sends him away. Dr Kenn notices how unhappy she looks and his sympathy is welcomed by Maggie who tells him she will soon be leaving St Ogg's for another teaching post. Lucy is very distressed to hear this news and wonders if this decision stems from Maggie's uncertainty over how much she loves Philip. Maggie assures her she would marry Philip if it were not for Tom's disapproval.

Commentary
The characters, in the setting of the bazaar, are vividly presented to us – we see what they do, hear what they say – but the reader is conscious of strong undercurrents. Maggie and Stephen have been 'dispensing with self-conquest' over the last few days; Maggie is 'a struggler still tossed by the waves'; Philip calls Stephen a hypocrite and neither he nor the reader can be sure whether the charge is unjustified; we discover Maggie has secretly organised her escape from her emotional and moral dilemma;

Lucy is stunned by the news and thinks of every reason but the real one.

Dr Kenn's perceptive sympathy contrasts with the shallow reactions of the social observers of the second paragraph. The suggestion that he can help Maggie not because he is a clergyman but because he belongs to a 'natural priesthood' reflects Eliot's own belief that religion stems from humanity's own noblest instincts.

In a typical passage Eliot urges the reader to work out why Maggie, having at last achieved the homage she has always desired – her motives for running away to the gypsies (Book 1, Chapter 11) are recalled – is yet so bitterly unhappy. The answer is not simple, and what is meant by the phrase 'passion, and affection' will only be fully explored in the final chapter of Book 6.

Book 6, Chapter 10 – The spell seems broken

Summary

The bazaar has been followed by a ball held by Stephen's sisters, the two Miss Guests. Stephen kisses Maggie and the act so shocks her that it restores her old self-control. The next morning she is able to assure Philip that the only reason she cannot marry him is Tom's disapprobation. Philip is not completely convinced.

Commentary

Maggie's ignorance of her own nature is full of danger: she thinks she is determined to renounce Stephen but allows herself to be with him alone in a place which looks 'enchanted', when dancing has made 'her whole frame set to joy', and where she speaks of her hunger for 'the half-opened rose' which makes her feel 'wicked'. What then shocks her is not so much Stephen's almost inevitable reaction, but the way this destroys her own vision of herself – his kiss has caused a 'leprosy': she will fling the affair 'away into an unvisited chamber of memory'. The violence of her virginal reaction means that she really believes what she says to Philip the next morning, though Philip's uncertainty echoes that of the reader.

Book 6, Chapter 11 – The lane

Summary

Maggie is spending a week with her Aunt Moss when Stephen appears and insists on talking to Maggie alone. He begs her to forget their old loyalties to Lucy and Philip and to marry him. He argues that neither of them can honestly give their love to anyone else, and that if Maggie really loved him she would abandon all other ties. Maggie is very moved but says that if they are guided only by their love they will make others miserable. She refuses to be the cause of such suffering.

Commentary
Maggie's agreement about the rightness of surrendering to love, except where others would be betrayed, reflects Eliot's deeply held opinion. She had condemned Jane Eyre's refusal to stay with Rochester (in Charlotte Brontë's novel) since their union would have harmed no one. There is, too, a more personal overtone. Eliot's own decision to live with Lewes, taken in the face of outraged social convention, was made possible because she knew no former partner would be emotionally hurt. Maggie and Stephen's situation is different.

Book 6, Chapter 12 – A family party

Summary
Maggie's visit to her Aunt Pullet is marked by a family party to celebrate Tom's acquisition of Dorlcote Mill, and Lucy persuades the aunts to give him some of their linen. She reveals to Tom how Philip has persuaded his father to sell the Mill thinking this will make him think more kindly of Philip possibly marrying Maggie. Tom, however, is obdurate in his opposition.

Commentary
Maggie's family regard her desire for independence as socially degrading and perverse, but for the reader this criticism is balanced by the eccentricities developed by those who stay at home – Aunt Pullet's keys and Aunt Glegg's mouldy furnishings. Tom and Lucy are seen together for the first time since childhood, and their characters are poles apart. Tom is 'good and upright' but rigidly prejudiced: he is incapable of 'the doubt-provoking knowledge we call truth'. Like Mrs Tulliver in Book 3, Chapter 7, Lucy has intervened without understanding the character of the man involved, and made things worse. Now Tom suspects Maggie's sincerity.

Book 6, Chapter 13 – Borne along by the tide

Summary
Maggie is spending her final days with Aunt Glegg but returning to Lucy's in the evenings. Stephen cannot keep away: he and Maggie long to be together before their final separation. Philip becomes certain that they are in love and arranges for Stephen to take his place in a boating expedition arranged for the next day, though he does not know that Lucy also is not going. After an initial reluctance, Maggie sets out with Stephen, but in the emotional intensity of their meeting neither notices when they reach Luckneth, where they were to have left the boat and walked back. When Stephen does notice he takes it as a sign that they should let the tide carry them on and elope together. Maggie is at first startled and

horrified, but then is persuaded by pity for Stephen's situation, and by the practical obstacles involved, to surrender to his plan. They are taken on board a passing Dutch steamer en route to Mudport and Maggie falls asleep on the deck.

Commentary
The problem here is to make the Victorian reader aware of the current of passionate sexual attraction between Maggie and Stephen without scandalising a family audience. Nowadays this presents little difficulty since explicit statement is uncensored and the characters themselves would be less bewildered by their dilemma. As it is, the ebb and flow between ethical considerations and sexual affinity is established by such means as Stephen's use of music to play upon Maggie, the attractiveness for Maggie of Stephen's care and in the second paragraph of the chapter the way in which the description of Maggie's heart-searching moves from authorial analysis to a broken indirect speech and then to exclamatory first person soliloquy. The dangers of the characters' indecision is metaphorically emphasised by their being adrift on the river.

Book 6, Chapter 14 - Waking

Summary
During the night Maggie dreams of Lucy, Philip and Tom. When she wakes she is appalled to realise how cruelly she has betrayed them. She resolves that she will part from Stephen and tells him this just before they disembark at Mudport. Stephen fiercely argues against her decision, urging the strength of their mutual love which would make any other marriage a mockery, that their flight has already decided the issue since Maggie is irremediably compromised, and that Maggie is now betraying him. But Maggie sees no happiness in their love because it would be founded on others' misery and her own selfishness. She leaves Stephen in the inn and boards the first stage coach she sees. This takes her still further away from home, to York, where she stays the night.

Commentary
Maggie's dream foreshadows her reconciliation with Tom through her death, but it also points to the forces that will make her rejection of happiness with Stephen inevitable. The Virgin/Lucy image is that of selfless and redeeming love while the confused Philip/Tom figure is an equally powerful image of duty. The day before Maggie had been 'robbed of choice' - now she will satisfy her conscience though she causes the maximum distress to Stephen and herself. Tom's gloomy suspicions about the perverseness of

Maggie's resolutions (end of Chapter 12) seem justified, specially when she accidentally takes a coach going in the wrong direction.

BOOK 7 THE FINAL RESCUE

Chapter 1 - Return to the Mill

Summary
Five days after her departure, Maggie returns to seek refuge with her brother at Dorlcote Mill. He refuses to shelter her but Mrs Tulliver will not desert her and accompanies her to Bob Jakin's house. Maggie asks Bob to contact Dr Kenn but finds this must be postponed since the latter's wife has just died.

Commentary
Maggie's return to Tom seems to symbolise a desire for punishment and is symptomatic of the strange relationship between these two. His rejection is a foretaste of the way the world will condemn Maggie. Mrs Tulliver, on the other hand, like Bob (and like Mumps) is only motivated by reasons of the heart. Notice the way the final dénouement is being prepared. Maggie must be near the river, yet not at the Mill.

Book 7, Chapter 2 - St Ogg's passes judgement

Summary
The first paragraph imagines the worldly-wise favourable reactions of St Ogg's if Maggie and Stephen had married and returned after a couple of months - the second reflects the censorious reactions to Maggie's actual unmarried return. Public opinion exonerates Stephen and condemns Maggie. Largely ignorant of the way she is regarded, Maggie visits Dr Kenn and tells him the full story. He informs her that Stephen, who is in Holland, has written to his father, completely exonerating Maggie. He suggests she leave St Ogg's but Maggie is determined to stay and Dr Kenn promises to help her, though he sees no easy way out.

Commentary
The reported voices of St Ogg's society provide a great deal of factual information as well as showing the reader how difficult Maggie's position will be. Dr Kenn here acts as a moral spokesman - he sees the possibility that for Stephen and Maggie to marry may possibly be the only social solution, but he rejects the responsibility of interference between Maggie and her conscience in 'the shifting relation between passion and duty'. The final paragraph with its gravely emphatic appraisal of how moral

judgements should be reached is in strong contrast with the feather-weight gossip of the opening.

Book 7, Chapter 3 – Showing that old acquaintances are capable of surprising us

Summary

Aunt Glegg, after hearing of Stephen's letter, comes to Maggie's defence offering her niece a home. She quarrels with Tom, who is more bitter about Maggie since he had once been so fond of her. Maggie is increasingly worried about Philip until she receives a letter from him. This assures her of his unchanged devotion.

Commentary

Maggie's disaster produces revealing reactions: Aunt Glegg's family loyalty, Mrs Tulliver's devotion to her children, Tom's rigidity, which seems to be intensified by an unacknowledged jealousy, and Philip's emotional and intellectual truth.

Book 7, Chapter 4 – Maggie and Lucy

Summary

Dr Kenn discovers that he cannot persuade any of his parishioners to employ Maggie as a governess or a companion, so decides to give Maggie charge of his own young children. St Ogg's is outraged and quickly suspects that they are likely to marry. Meanwhile Maggie yearns for news of Lucy, who, she hears, has recovered from her initial shock sufficiently to be going on holiday with the Miss Guests to recuperate and possibly meet Stephen again. One evening Lucy appears for a brief secret visit and the two cousins are reunited: Maggie assures Lucy that Stephen will one day come back to her.

Commentary

There are more contrasted interpretations of Maggie's behaviour – the scandalised voyeuristic reaction of the majority of St Ogg's, the moral timidity of the minority, and the Miss Guests' suspicion are in sharp distinction to Lucy's affection. As with Philip's letter in the previous chapter, Lucy's trust makes Maggie's renunciation more comprehensible – and her final unfinished sentence underlines the heroism of that renunciation.

Book 7, Chapter 5 – The last conflict

Summary

Dr Kenn, warned of the gossip about himself and Maggie, unwillingly ends her employment, promising to find her work elsewhere. A letter from Stephen begs her to end his misery by summoning him and his despair tempts her to do so, until she thinks of Lucy and Philip. She burns Stephen's letter and is praying for strength when she realises water is flooding into the house, heavy rainstorms having made the Floss burst its banks. After rousing Bob, Maggie takes one of the boats to row to Dorlcote Mill fearing they are in danger there. After great difficulty she reaches it and rescues Tom. They are almost in safety when a mass of wreckage overwhelms the boat and brother and sister are drowned.

Commentary

The catastrophe happens with a rapidity that startled early reviewers but there is a sense in which the flood supplies the only possible solution to Maggie's dilemma. The letter from Stephen shows her she will never finally be safe from that temptation (notice the questions in her prayer) and Dr Kenn has made it clear that she will only find work away from St Ogg's. Her longing for death, as a welcome relief, is echoed by her cry on the dark waters, 'Which is the way home?' Above all, her heroic rescue effects the reconciliation between Maggie and Tom: he can no longer doubt her now.

Conclusion

Five years later most of the damage is repaired. Tom and Maggie's grave is visited often by Philip, who never marries, and by Stephen who is later reconciled with Lucy. (See also section 5.5.)

4 THEMES AND ISSUES

4.1 ROMANTIC FASCINATION WITH THE CHILD

The first third of the novel (up to the closing of the 'golden gates' at the end of Book 2) revolves round Maggie and Tom's childhood and this portrayal, with its uncanny ability to enter into the mind of children, is probably the most successful part of the book. 'Child life in all its prosaic reality' said *The Times* and other reviewers hailed Eliot's ability to break away from the literary stereotypes of children, specially in the context of much contemporary didactic literature, with its crude contrasts of naughty (hell-bent) and good (dying young and going to heaven like Eva in *Uncle Tom's Cabin*). Eliot's intimate, exact and unsentimental study of children is a manifestation of the fascination with the young that was initiated by Rousseau.

Jean-Jacques Rousseau (1712–78)

Eliot once said it was worth learning French just to read Rousseau – he sent 'an electric thrill through my intellectual and moral frame'. This was not because she always agreed with him, but because he stimulated her into rethinking 'old prejudices'. This French philosopher was a seminal figure of the Romantic Movement, teaching that virtue was linked with the beauty of the natural world and that passion, if sincere, was innocent and good. He also held an almost mystic belief in the sacred quality of childhood, and in 1762 published a treatise on education called *Emile*. This demanded respect for children as children instead of treating them as embryo adults. Before this, educational methods had depended on the belief that the child's mind was an empty page upon which teachers should impress ideas in order to fashion a useful member of society. This was anathema to Rousseau who believed that 'there is no original sin in the human heart' and that vice only entered in through the bungling interference of teachers. So the child was to be left free to discover reality, specially through experience and through the senses rather than through words. Indeed, the only book allowed was to be Daniel Defoe's novel *Robinson Crusoe*, which Rousseau regarded as an exemplar of learning through experience. This 'charter of youthful deliverance' aroused enormous enthusiasm - 200 treatises on *Emile* were published in England before 1800; Rousseau's influence on the way people hereafter thought about children was profound, though the effect on education was often the reverse of what he had intended.

Eliot's account of childhood illustrates the way Rousseau inspired but certainly did not dominate her thinking. Perhaps the closest agreement comes in her account of the ludicrously unsuitable education Tom is given. Tom is the kind of boy who lives through his senses - 'he's got a notion of things out o' door, an' a sort of commonsense' says his father (Book 1, Chapter 3). Indeed, he has sharper perception than Mr Stelling - 'he could predict with accuracy what number of horses were cantering behind him, he could guess to a fraction how many lengths of his stick it would take to reach across the playground.' But the well-meaning Mr Stelling's ideas of education totally ignore his pupil's natural gifts. The regimen of Latin grammar and Euclid results in Tom having to pick up 'a promiscuous education from things that were not intended as education at all' (Book 2, Chapter 4).

The deficiency in Maggie's upbringing is different. We are told virtually nothing about her formal education, but her home subjects her to constant frustrations: she longs for love and admiration and hungers for the kind of material upon which her alert imagination can work. But Tom snubs her and her mother labours to make her resemble Lucy. Maggie is first seen lost in reverie by the water-wheel - it is typical that her mother summons her in and tries (in vain) to make her do her patchwork: her dangerous frustration is illustrated by her violence to the doll - 'alternatively grinding or beating the wooden head' against a brick wall. Yet the two children do survive their traumas and this is for the Rousseau-esqùe reason that they can wander at will in the natural world as, for instance, the final paragraph of Book 1, Chapter 5 describes: 'Tom thought people were at a disadvantage who lived on any other spot of the globe . . . Maggie thought it would make a very nice heaven to sit by the pool.'

Neither Maggie nor Tom, however, are in accord with Rousseau's idealised conception of childhood. Both have within them strong characteristics which seem to have developed as a bird's wing grows inside its shell - Tom's 'rigid, inflexible purposes' and Maggie's furies and hunger for admiration. Indeed, Tom is reported as trying to intimidate the sheep while still wearing his baby bonnets. Eliot refuses to portray them 'in the abstract, existing solely to illustrate the events of a mistaken education . . . but made of flesh and blood, with dispositions not entirely at the mercy of circumstances' (Book 2, Chapter 4). What links her with Rousseau is not her ideas about childhood, but the fascinated respect with which she studies it, her accurate graphing of the genetic imprints each child manifests and her demonstration of the relevance of their childhood at Dorlcote Mill to what happens in later years: all this is a tribute from the nineteenth-century novelist to the early Romantic, Rousseau.

William Wordsworth (1770–1850)

Rousseau's belief in the unique, intuitive understanding of the child and the danger of corrupting it by set teaching pervades Wordsworth's poetry. Most famous is his vision of the newborn child:

> trailing clouds of glory do we come
> From God, who is our home:
> Heaven lies about us in our infancy!
> Shades of the prison-house begin to close
> Upon the growing Boy . . .
> (Immortality Ode 1803)

Wordsworth repeatedly turns to look at childhood to try and understand what it is that matters in life and how (or if) this can be sustained. His great poetical autobiography *The Prelude*, published just after his death, traces how his ability to write poetry was moulded by his childhood and youth in the freedom of his Cumberland home. This is a most vivid evocation of his boyhood - bird-nesting on a rocky cliff face, rowing at night while the mountains gaze down at him, flying through the 'darkness and the cold' as he skates down Windermere, and he sadly contrasts the value of this freedom with the formalism and 'seemliness' of modern education.

Eliot read Wordsworth throughout her life and her belief that it is only by studying what is growing that we can understand the grown agrees exactly with his 'The child is father of the man'. Like him (and Rousseau) she found her 'roots of piety' in the lovely countryside of her childhood and gives Tom and Maggie and their father the same formative influence, though she is unlike Wordsworth, who remembered childhood with nostalgic yearning: she thought it only happy in retrospect - 'to the child it is full of deep sorrows'.

Charles Dickens and Charlotte Brontë

No one more profoundly influenced the Victorian reading public's attitude to children than Dickens. His own traumatic experience when he was left to fend for himself in London at the age of 12 so penetrated his consciousness that nearly every book has its desolate child, at the mercy of the cruelty, stupidity or greed of adults or subjected by them to a deforming education. The first English novel to centre on a child hero is his *Oliver Twist* (1837): with *David Copperfield* (1849) (which Tolstoy put as the apex of European novel writing) he was able to exorcise some of his own childhood misery.

Charlotte Brontë's *Jane Eyre* (1847) similarly carries both the factual details and emotional intensity which show that fiction marches side by side with unhappy autobiography. The death of her mother and of two belovèd older sisters at a harsh boarding school had scarred her childhood. In *Jane Eyre*, a novel of almost hypnotic power which became an immediate best-seller, the world is seen exclusively through the eyes of the cruelly victimised child-heroine, isolated in a world as grotesquely dangerous as that of a fairy tale. *David Copperfield* and *Jane Eyre* have close similarities: they are both written in the first person with the fictional hero looking back on the younger self, both are orphans, both have unhappy childhoods deprived of love and are sent to savage schools. Both find their only solace in books and undergo a traumatic journey by themselves into an unknown world. Above all, the sympathy of the reader is insistently directed towards the child at the centre of the novel.

It is not surprising that when *The Mill on the Floss* appeared reviewers immediately thought of these two books in comparison – but it is very different. Young Maggie and Tom are placed firmly at the centre of interest and sympathy in the book, but their childhood is given an idyllic Wordsworthian setting and each has the unreserved love of at least one parent. Intentional cruelty is unknown to the Tulliver household and no one goes hungry. What Eliot does in this unpromisingly pleasant environment is to demonstrate how, even so, Maggie suffers bitter anguish because she does not fit her mother's and brother's expectations and how Tom is subjected, with the best intentions, to the most unsuitable education. There is no need for cruel guardians or harsh schools: an unequally divided jampuff, straight hair or a father's ambition will do. Moreover, the children are presented in no idealised fashion: Tom is as stiff-necked and self-satisfied as his Aunt Glegg and Maggie as imprudent as her father. When she runs away to the gypsies, there is an echo of little David Copperfield's flight from London – but he is the helpless victim of circumstance, whereas Maggie is partly inspired by the hope that at last she will receive the admiration she feels she deserves. With the Tulliver children, the Romantic interest in the child reaches a new exactness of unsentimental observation.

Elizabeth Gaskell: The Moorland Cottage

A tale by Mrs Gaskell, *The Moorland Cottage* (1851) is also worth comparing with *The Mill on the Floss*, since it too is the study of a strongly contrasted brother and sister who grow up in the country, the sister is called Maggie and the story ends with the brother drowning and the sister only being rescued in the nick of time. The characters are, however, the merest puppets, illustrating the results of sound religious teaching on the girl and a foolish mother on the boy. This Maggie is unbelievably self-sacrificing and forgiving under all circumstances while Edward, the brother, goes to the bad with melodramatic thoroughness. Mrs Gaskell herself called it a 'worthless tale' (she wrote an incomparably better study of childhood later in *Wives and Daughters*), but it is no worse than the hundreds of Sunday School 'Reward' books being poured out in the mid nineteenth century and its simplificiations of character and motive and its religiosity provide a useful contrast to the complex reality of the Tulliver children.

The 'emergent self'

Eliot's recall of her own 'remotest past' is evidenced in her sonnet sequence *Brother and Sister* (section 1.2) and it is the joys and miseries of her relationship with Isaac that gives the account of Tom and Maggie's growing up such authenticity. Maggie's earliest memory is 'standing with Tom by the side of the Floss while he held my hand' (Book 5, Chapter 1). Later on, the reader is told 'To have no cloud between herself and Tom was still a perpetual yearning in her, that had its root deeper than all change' (Book 6, Chapter 12).

Maggie's inability to escape this 'yearning' provides the emotional core of the book but it is not the only reflection of the theme of the 'emergent self'. Eliot's letters indicate that Tom too must be understood in terms of his childhood; Mr Tulliver's childhood memories of his mother, so like 'the little wench', and of his father carry the seeds of his future life: 'My father was a huge man for planting . . . and I used to follow him about like a dog', and as Tulliver looks at the orchard and the malthouse his father built, he sees the roots of his being and knows in any other place 'I should go off my head . . . I should be like as if I'd lost my way.' His love for Dorlcote Mill is as essential to him as Tom is to Maggie: 'He knew the sound of every gate and door . . . every roof and weather stain and broken hillock was good because his growing senses had been fed on them' (Book 3, Chapter 9).

4.2 THE DUTY OF THE ARTIST: THE IMPOSSIBILITY OF MORAL JUDGEMENTS

Eliot intellectually rejected Evangelical Christianity but never challenged its concepts of duty, moral choice and the rejection of self-indulgence. As an artist her supreme purpose is ethical, and she saw her duty plainly: 'to call forth judgement, pity and sympathy', by showing life, not as it ideally should be, but as she found it really exemplified in human behaviour. Her rejection of idealism upset many conventional readers - they called *The Mill on the Floss* 'inimical', worried that this 'passionately written presentment of temptation never conquered' would influence people for the bad; the critic Ruskin called the characters 'the sweepings out of a Pentonville omnibus'. For Eliot, however, moral duty demanded that she did not falsify observed life into a moral parable or a comfortably happy ending. Towards the end of the novel she demonstrates the unlikelihood, indeed the impossibility, of such an 'end to the story', by letting Lucy try to persuade Tom 'to turn completely round' (Book 6, Chapter 12). Lucy's inevitable failure reflects how any easy solution is out of the question not only for the obstinate Tom but for Maggie and Stephen and ironically, for reasons Lucy has yet no suspicion of, for Lucy herself.

This moral duty to the truth is linked with that reverence for life she had found for instance in Strauss, with his insistence that 'Man is the true Incarnation'. The novelist must do all in her power to enlarge sympathy, because 'our moral progress may be measured by the degree in which we sympathise with individual suffering and individual joy', and it is typical that Philip's last letter to Maggie names 'the enlarged life which grows and grows by appropriating the life of others' as her most precious gift to him. Now this enlarged sympathy is totally at odds with the concept of absolute moral laws. Like the great German poet, Goethe, Eliot thought that the idea of people being either good or bad was an 'immoral fiction'. Every case, every circumstance is different and must be comprehended, not judged according to a set of maxims: there is 'no master key that will fit all cases' she says, just after presenting the St Ogg's judgement on Maggie with such contemptuous irony, 'the mysterious complexity of our life is not to be embraced by maxims' lacking the 'wide fellow feeling with all that is human' (Book 7, Chapter 2).

4.3 *THE MILL ON THE FLOSS* AS SOCIAL HISTORY

The world Eliot presents is that of country and small provincial town, exactly the environment of the first twenty years of her own life. It is a claustrophobic society, ignorant of the outside world, tenacious of prejudice, custom, and property, materialistic but commercially timid and without any manifestations of artistic or intellectual activity. Women's life is even more restricted than men's: Mrs Tulliver immerses herself in housekeeping. Mrs Pullet's hobby is her own and her neighbours' health, though Mrs Glegg, unusually, is allowed by her husband to manage her own money. Education is a 'chancy' business - even when conscientiously administered, it is confined to classics and mathematics, taking no account of natural aptitudes or intended career. Academic education is expensive and not for girls.

Changes were imminent, however, and as the years slip by in the novel, even St Ogg's alters. Mr Deane notes how much quicker Tom can rise in business than himself when young, and Guest & Co.'s business flourishes greatly. There is a suggestion that steam-power be used for Dorlcote Mill. The newly-appointed Dr Kenn is a very different sort of clergyman from his predecessor. The purpose of the bazaar of Book 6 is to build and endow schools. By the end of the book, the younger characters are in a changing society, but it is still one hostile to unconventionality. Maggie's desire for economic independence is regarded as wayward and her nonconformity with sexual mores renders her a social outcast.

4.4 THE INDIVIDUAL AND SOCIETY

Shortly before writing *The Mill on the Floss* Eliot had re-read Greek drama and spoke of Sophocles' 'delineation of primitive emotions' as a major influence upon her. In an 1856 essay on his play *Antigone* she discussed 'the struggle between elemental tendencies and established laws . . . Wherever the strength of a man's intellect, or moral sense or affection brings him into opposition with the rules which society has sanctioned, *there* is the conflict renewed!' In Wordsworth, too, whose poetry she read throughout her life, she found the same tension between two worlds – between the eighteenth-century faith that rationality and control were the means to build a good society and the Romantic insistence on individual freedom, on the 'holiness of the heart's affections' [John Keats] and on the menace presented to these by the entrenched power of religious and political establishments.

This dilemma between social duty and private feeling, between head and heart, surfaces in all Eliot's novels, and here the clash between Tom and Maggie is the opposition between conformist and individualist. When children, they are sometimes shown like 'two friendly ponies', but already Tom's strong orientation to order and authority is sharply in contrast with Maggie whose 'moral sense or affection' continually brings her 'into opposition with the rules which society has sanctioned'. Society's rules vary in her case from how her hair should look, to whether she should earn her living, and what is proper behaviour between men and women, and is represented by Tom, by the Dodson aunts and by St Ogg's. Maggie's father is an individualist like herself, and demonstrates just how disastrous it can be to have such a 'contrairy' temperament. To some extent, Philip, Lucy and Dr Kenn act as intermediaries between the two extremes. From the tension between conformist and individualist stems

Maggie's sad inability to have the relationship with Tom which eludes her throughout the novel and also her struggle between loyalty to Lucy and Philip and her passion for Stephen.

4.5 RELIGIOUS CLIMATE

Provincial England, into which Eliot was born, regarded religion very much as the Tullivers and Dodsons did: 'Their belief in the unseen, so far as it manifests itself at all, seems to be rather of a pagan kind: their moral notions, though held with strong tenacity, seem to have no standard beyond hereditary custom' (Book 4, Chapter 1). A conventional Anglicanism was undisturbed by either spiritual fervour or religious doubt. Most people would agree with Mr Tulliver that 'the church was one thing and common sense another': Sunday church-going and similar junketings bore no relationship to the real business of life, which was 'to be honest and rich, and not only rich but richer than was supposed'. Roman Catholicism was thought of as a strange aberration, connected with wicked foreigners; the reforming zeal of the eighteenth-century John Wesley was largely forgotten and his followers had settled down into their own tightly-organised chapel-going communities, their dissent (from Anglicanism) being regarded as 'a foolish habit . . . which appeared to run in families like asthma'.

Yet a reforming vigour had already appeared in the Church at the beginning of the nineteenth century with the Evangelical movement. This was characterised by a tireless social conscience, producing reformers like William Wilberforce and Lord Shaftesbury, famous for their work against the slave trade and inhuman factory conditions, respectively. Equally characteristic was its revulsion against any laxness in personal morals, its insistence on personal holiness, on rigorous self-examination, its seriousness and indeed its narrow-mindedness. Though Eliot's father resembled Mr Tulliver in his attitude to religion, she herself was attracted in her teens by the fervous of Evangelicalism: a Methodist aunt and two of her school mistresses influenced her, but the rigour of her puritanism soon exceeded that of her teachers. The theatre, oratorios, novel-reading, even parts of Shakespeare, were all condemned by the nineteen-year-old girl.

By 1839 she had moved away from this extreme position. It had, however, marked her with an ineradicable sense of duty, a belief in the need for self-conquest and the purifying effect of human trials, an awareness of the tension between the ideal and the real – and the feeling that the latter must be endured 'without opium'. All her writing would carry these hallmarks of the Evangelical temper, and we can clearly see how they affect the presentation of Maggie.

While Evangelicalism was successfully reactivating the Anglican conscience, traditional Christianity was faced by two formidable intellectual challenges. The first was a vigorous effort, particularly by German scholars, to disentangle reliable historical elements in the evolution of Christianity from accretion of myth. The resultant spring-cleaning of the gospels and the history of the primitive church left many believers aghast: miraculous elements were discounted, much of the narrative being seen, not as conscious deception, but as the self-delusion of devoted followers. Two of these seminal books were translated into English by Eliot herself, Strauss's *Life of Christ* (1846) and Feuerbach's *Essence of Christianity* (1854). After exhaustive textual criticism, the former suggests that the Scriptures are myths, that is, imaginative symbols for the 'deepest philosophical truth – that Man is the true Incarnation'. Feuerbach develops this humanistic concept and his belief that man had created God from his own inner nature profoundly affected Eliot and the way she wrote novels. Her demand for sympathy, not judgement (see section 4.2) is an echo of Feuerbach: 'Without other men the world would be not only dead and empty but meaningless. Only through his fellow does man become clear to himself and self-conscious but only when I am clear to myself does the world become clear to me.'

The second challenge to traditional Christianity came from the work of biologists and geologists. This showed conclusively that the Genesis creation story was a myth and the neat time scheme taught in schools and printed in bibles which dated the fall of Adam and Eve at 4004 BC, would have to go and with it many other old, comfortable certainties.

Some reacted by deciding – like Newman – to opt out of such intellectual dilemmas by joining the Catholic Church with its claim to infallibility, or strove – like Pusey and Dr Kenn in this novel – to introduce a more decisive authority into the Anglican Church. Others reacted, like Eliot, by accepting the force of empirical evidence with relief. 'The choice of good for its own sake', without the threat of eternal damnation was her ideal. She wrote to her father that though she admired and cherished the moral teachings of Jesus himself, she considered the Church's consequent development of a 'system of doctrines . . . pernicious in its influence on individual and social happiness'.

The Mill on the Floss inevitably carries the impression of these religious crosscurrents. There is the accurate picture of the torpid conventionality of St Ogg's and the inability of the new vicar Dr Kenn to persuade his parishioners to live their lives in terms of their professed religion. Maggie's religious awakening and her attempts to achieve self-renunciation recall her creator's own fervour at the same age, while Philip's warning of the dangers of such 'self-delusive fanaticism' reflects the reasoning which led her to turn away from her own fanatically puritan phase. Maggie, of course, would know nothing of the intellectual reasons which led Eliot away from conventional Christianity.

Finally, there is a reflection in the novel of the insistent self-examination of the Evangelical. Perhaps no other novelist has such an acute moral sensibility, particularly concerning the ingenuity of self-deception and the intricacy of motivation. Why Riley recommends Stelling, why Tulliver changes his mind about Gritty's loan, why Tom interrupts Philip's singing, why Wakem employs Tulliver, why Maggie goes into the conservatory with Stephen – the novel is shot through with moral problems for the reader to work upon. In her insistence that the reader cease to be passive and assume instead an active self-educating role, she resembles those two other great novelists, Thomas Hardy and D. H. Lawrence. David Cecil said no one ever showed more vividly 'the process of moral defeat . . . With an inexorable clearness she reveals how temptation insinuates itself into the mind, how it retreats at the first suspicious movement of conscience, how it comes back disguised . . . it will sham death only to arise suddenly and sweep its victim away . . . Maggie's passion for Stephen steals into her inexperienced mind, imperceptibly, so that she only realises it when it has become such an obsession that she is unable to see it in its true proportions' (*Early Victorian Novelists*).

Eliot's exact analysis derives from the Evangelical's strict examination of conscience as much as her open-minded, sympathetic compassion relates to her rejection of dogmatic religious judgements.

4.6 SCIENTIFIC IDEAS

In the nineteenth century scientists and imaginative writers still used the same mutually comprehended language, a situation unlike the 'two cultures' of today. Darwin took the poems of John Milton with him on the voyage of the Beagle and we know that from the age of twenty, Eliot read every scientific book that came her way. Her association with the *Westminster Review* and then with Lewes, who was primarily a scientific journalist, meant she was aware of the most recent scientific ideas of the day. She had read Darwin's *The Origin of Species* within a few days of publication and, in a letter to a friend, welcomed it as a further exemplification of the doctrine of development – that is, the belief that the universe was in a continuous state of evolution instead of being created, whole and entire, at a single moment of time. It was felt that the discovery of the laws governing this evolution was now possible through empiric science and these would point the way to social improvement, a belief reflected in the great popularity, not only of books on natural history, geology and archaeology, but also those on the evolution of society. This scientific climate of ideas had a profound influence on Eliot, and can be seen in the narrative structure, characterisation, themes and images of *The Mill on the Floss*. In absorbing these contemporary ideas on evolutionary theory and transmuting them into the imaginative and emotional life of the novels, she exercised a seminal influence on her period.

In an 1876 letter she defined her writing in a scientific phrase: 'a set of experiments in life' and justified this by arguing that theories and formulae led to misleading simplifications, but that the novelist's art, which relates theory to individual human experience, would not mislead. The phrase 'set of experiments' is interesting in relation to the organisation of narrative in *The Mill on the Floss*. The reader notices how uneven is the length of the seven books, varying between three and fourteen chapters, and equally noticeable are its omissions. There is a lot about Tom at Mr Stelling's but nothing about Maggie at Miss Firmiss's boarding school. Neither Maggie nor Tom is seen at their respective jobs, Lucy remains off-stage in Books 2 to 5 and reappears in Book 6, when Stephen also appears, and Tom seems eclipsed.

However, any scientist knows experiments need to be selective and are also quite unpredictable in length. Maggie's experiment with the gypsies needs less than an afternoon, but it is one of a series illustrating the frustration of her natural bent and so forms one chapter in a book. Her religious conversion spans a couple of years but it is completed without major plot implication so it forms a book by itself. Each book centres on a mutating process sometimes successful, like Maggie's increased self-awareness in Book 4, or the effect on Maggie of Philip's articulate intelligence in Book 5, or unsuccessful, as in Book 2, where Tom's expensive education fails to touch his intellect or his 'Rhadamanthine' prejudices, or in Books 1 and 3 which concern Mr Tulliver's inability to adapt. He is a fascinating case, for two processes are at work upon him: the wife he chose because of her stupidity and the times which, as Mr Deane points out, are changing. The effect of the first is irrational action, since he always acts against her wishes, even when they are reasonable, as in begging him not to go to law; the changing times affect him in matters concerning the water-power by which five generations of his family have earned their living. The problem is not a difficult one - Mr Deane suggests steam-power as a possibility - but Tulliver is incapable of change and only reacts with ruinous law suits, loud anger and a curse inscribed in the family bible. As for his final act, both Tom (Book 5, Chapter 7) and Wakem (Book 6, Chapter 8) reasonably describe it as madness, and his dying words are those of one unable to adapt to his changing environment and therefore doomed.

His story is tragic, but inability to adapt can also be comic, and on the periphery of the book are several characters of this kind, such as Stelling (who will never get his deanery), the Gleggs and the Pullets; it is perhaps significant that both the latter are barren. At the centre of the book is Maggie and her painful adaptations or failures to adapt to the life around her. Book 6 is a very explosive experiment indeed with the unpredictable possibilities of mixing a Maggie and a Stephen. But the situation is made more complex because of the other elements present - Maggie's childhood relationship to Tom, Philip's influence, and her conviction of the prime duty of loyalty if any good society is to be preserved. It is not surprising that reviewers were indignant that the upshot is fudged by a melodramatic drowning since the results of this final experiment, so to speak, have been ruined by breaking the specimen slide. Only Dr Kenn's objective consideration of Stephen's letter suggests how adaptation and survival might have been managed - a possibility the reader is left to consider on his own.

Early in Book 1 Mr Tulliver laments the unpredictable results of 'crossing breeds' and the themes of breeding, genetic descent, inherited characteristics and kinship recur throughout the novel. Mrs Tulliver and her sisters never cease to bewail the difference in Dodson and Tulliver strains. Philip Wakem takes after his mother but Tom's steady dislike of him reflects a typical inability to accept the importance of female genes as well as an atavistic horror of possibly mingling his blood, through Maggie, with anything crippled. Tom takes after his mother's side, even to liking a lot of salt in his soup. The problem then arises - if heredity conditions us, have we free will? - and this is why people's complex motivations so fascinated Eliot.

Images derived from science permeate the novel, and all readers discover their own examples. The failure of religion to influence Mr Tulliver is compared with the failure of those seeds lacking 'an apparatus of hooks' to get a hold on unreceptive surfaces (Book 4, Chapter 1). Mr Stelling's unsuitable educational methods for Tom are like a beaver determined to build the same dam whether he is in a Canadian river or in a London bedroom (Book 2, Chapter 1). The attention given to the 'emmet-like' Dodsons is justified by the way natural science demonstrates that every particle of evidence contributes to the understanding of the whole (Book 4, Chapter 1). When St Ogg's is described (Book 1, Chapter 12), its history and that of the human society it serves is compared not only with bower birds and white ants but with tree markings. Mr Glegg occupies spare hours by reflecting impartially on 'zoological phenomena' and the 'contrairiness' of his wife. Images as well as themes, characters and the organisation of narrative are linked to the potent influence of Victorian scientific thinking.

4.7 THE POSITION OF WOMEN

The 'woman question' was the subject of lively debate all through the nineteenth century: the role of woman in society, her duties to her family, how she should be educated, what political and legal rights she should have, what the ideal woman was like. Eliot was well aware of the difficulties faced by women, specially those less gifted than herself: a character in her novel *Felix Holt* comments 'God was cruel when he made women', and the opening of Book 5, Chapter 2 presents them in the traditionally helpless, passive role 'with streaming hair and uplifted hands, offering prayers, watching the world's combat from afar, filling their long empty days with memories and fears'. This picture is then ironically linked with Maggie, whose fate is similarly restricted by the hampering expectations of her society while Tom is free to join in the 'hurrying ardour of action'.

Maggie is much 'sharper' than Tom, yet it is taken for granted that Tom is the one to have the expensive education, the imbalance being reflected in the proportionate space given in the novel to the description of each child's schooling. Mr Stelling assures her that girls are superficial – 'quick and shallow'. Maggie has smaller Christmas-boxes than Tom simply because, as the latter explains, he is a boy. When disaster strikes, Tom's energy in making money earns approval from all and he is able to do so successfully: Maggie has to stay at home, sewing, and when she attempts to assist the family finances by selling this modest ability Tom is angry because she thus endangers their social status. When Maggie and Philip's meetings in the Red Deeps are discovered by Tom, he assumes the right to judge and punish and Maggie has no alternative but obedience because 'you are a man, Tom, and have power, and can do something in the world'.

After her father's death, Maggie, determined to be independent, has to work in a 'dreary situation' in a 'third-rate schoolroom': her only alternative is 'to live with Aunt Pullet', a daunting prospect. When she returns to St Ogg's unmarried after the disastrous river expedition, even though Stephen writes home exonerating her from all blame, the society of St Ogg's, which is in effect Maggie's world, condemns the woman and excuses the man: 'a young man of five and twenty is not to be severely judged in these cases – he is really very much at the mercy of a bold designing girl' (Book 7, Chapter 2). So the dearth of educational and professional opportunity, the resulting difficulty of achieving economic independence, the existence of a double sexual standard and the persistence of the idea of woman as temptress in any sexual situation – all these are shown as making life hard for the eager Maggie. She lives in a man's world, where women must, in Mr Tulliver's phrase, 'know their place' and Wakem, even more bleakly, only asks whom they belong to.

However, Eliot never over-simplifies Maggie's situation by suggesting that the social conditions of her time are the only formative influences upon her. Equally powerful are what she once called the 'non-moral, zoological facts of woman's nature,' presented in this novel mainly through the sustained contrast between Maggie's and Tom's innate qualities. Tom's desire to punish, for instance, is described as a typical boy's quality and later on he assumes the saturnine sternness of premature responsibility 'as a young man is likely to do' (Book 5, Chapter 2). When Mr Tulliver comes downstairs for the first time after his stroke, Tom is embarrassed by his pity 'like a true boy' while her father's weakness only intensifies Maggie's natural tenderness. Tom's rigidity of purpose is constantly at odds with Maggie's volatility. This is associated, when she is a little girl, with a propensity to tears and temper and a possessive jealousy, and later with emotional dependence, precipitancy, inconsistency – a characteristic which particularly irritates Tom – and a hunger for affection, and approval. The tomboy element of her girlhood, which Mrs Tulliver so deplores, only throws her unlikeness to a real boy, Tom, into sharper relief, and the reader knows it is Lucy, pretty as a picture, that Maggie longs to resemble. That Maggie's innate qualities are far from easy for her to cope with is the clear message of the book, and it is interesting how often in moments of turmoil Eliot signals her sympathy with her heroine by her choice of image: Maggie shows 'childlike relief' when Dr Kenn appears at the Bazaar, and 'childlike contrition' to Philip. The reader is reminded of Maggie's continuing emotional vulnerability throughout the novel both as child and adult.

Maggie's distress as she tries to be faithful to her own moral perception, and to discover an adequate outlet for her affections, intelligence and energy is thus linked by her creator with her nature as a woman as well as with her environment.

5 STYLE AND TECHNIQUE

5.1 DIALECT

When Lewes was encouraging Eliot to start writing novels he told her: 'You have wit, description and philosophy' – he only feared she lacked 'the highest quality of fiction – dramatic presentation'. He could not have been more wrong – it was discovered that Eliot had a remarkable gift of catching nuance of character in tone of voice. She had always admired writers who dared to be 'thoroughly familiar . . . like Shakespeare, Fielding, Scott and indeed every other writer of fiction of the first class . . . Shakespeare is intensely colloquial. One hears the very accent of living men'.

To capture this accent she drew richly from the voices she had heard in her childhood when she went round the neighbouring farms and sales with her father or listened to her aunts. Indeed she complained later of the difficulty of writing her historical novel *Romola* because she could not 'hear' the language of her characters in the way that her memory made Tulliver and Dodson voices vividly present to her. Sound, turn of phrase, vocabulary make the family conferences crackle with hostile innuendo. Sometimes the effect comes from a loosely constructed sentence which reaches an unexpected but revealing conclusion, as when Tulliver explains to Riley the education he wants for Tom: 'I want him to know figures and write like print and see into things quick and know what folks mean and how to wrap things up in words as aren't actionable' (Book 1, Chapter 3).

The conversation between Aunt Glegg and Aunt Pullet on the dropsical 'old Mrs Sulton o' the Twenty lands' (Book 1, Chapter 7) instantly characterises the two sisters and is very funny, as are Mrs Tulliver's reflections on: 'them best Holland sheets, I should repent buying 'em, only they'll do to lay us out in. And if you was to die tomorrow, Mr Tulliver, they're mangled beautiful, an' all ready' (Book 1, Chapter 2).

But the use of the country voice can equally be very moving, as when Mr Tulliver lies dying, or when his poor wife laments that all her household treasures are to be sold and tries to persuade her sister Deane to buy her belovèd silver teapot at the auction:

> I should be so loth for 'em to buy it at the Golden Lion . . . my tea pot as I bought when I was married, and to think o' its being scratched and set before travellers and folks - and my letters on it - see here - E.D. - and everybody to see 'em. (Book 3, Chapter 3).

Country dialect also has its uses as a thermometer of social differences - this is clear in the Tulliver-Riley dialogue and when Mrs Tulliver goes to visit Lawyer Wakem. It also operates strongly to draw a line between Bob Jakin and Maggie. It is an educational differential too - Mr Deane does not talk like the other uncles for he has taken pains with his social demeanour 'in his upward process' and Tom's speech, even before he goes to Mr Stelling, is unlike Bob's, who adds to a strong Midlands accent a fascinating habit of refrain in his verbs: 'He's the biggest rot-catcher anywhere - he is. I'd sooner be a rot-catcher nor anything - I would' (Book 2, Chapter 6).

It is a little surprising indeed that Tom and Maggie, even in their earliest days, seem to speak in Standard English, this difference suggesting a definite divide between old and young, past and future. In some novels Eliot uses the consciousness of dialect to indicate snobbery or pretension, but the only manifestation here is perhaps the 'vulgarity' of Lucy's relations which 'made the Miss Guests shudder a little'.

5.2 THE AUTHORIAL VOICE

A characteristic of Eliot's style is her easy colloquy with the reader. This has been out of fashion for most of this century but it is ludicrous to be aggrieved at hearing the author's voice speaking directly or to pretend that the story has an independent existence. In his final letter to Maggie, Philip speaks of: 'that enlarged life which grows and grows by appropriating the life of others' (Book 7, Chapter 3), and it is Eliot's constant endeavour to involve the reader's own experience into the moral understanding of the book. This can take the form of making the reader share the problems of the writer as in the discussion of how far character and how far circumstances control our lives (Book 6, Chapter 6) or in clarifying present events by reference to the long perspective of history (Book 4, Chapter 1; Book 1, Chapter 12). Sometimes the question is actually explicit as though the reader is enquiring - when Maggie is discovered in a state of feverish excitement after her first evening with Stephen: 'Had anything remarkable happened?' (Book 6, Chapter 3), and Eliot goes on to analyse what was in fact 'remarkable' that evening in Maggie's terms. Much more briefly at the end of the same chapter she firmly calls the readers' attention to a subtlety they might have missed, as Maggie herself may have done, that her confession to Lucy is true, but incomplete, since she has not mentioned the impact upon her of Lucy's own love, Stephen. Sometimes she observes the difference between appearance and reality – as in the contrast between Tom's agreeably boyish appearance and the 'rigid inflexible purpose' this conceals, generalising this to invoke the reader's own observation (Book 1, Chapter 5). Sometimes she addresses the reader directly: this happens in the very first chapter, establishing an intimate assumption of the readers' sympathy with the shared memory of things past – she does this again when, after a lapse of years, we see Maggie walking down to the Red Deeps. 'You may see her', says Eliot, and goes on to paint a picture of the now beautiful seventeen-year-old as she stands among the firs. But this is not an ornamental passage – the writer has halted the narration to make the reader notice the danger inherent in so young a face apparently subdued into so old a quietude.

Just occasionally the author's voice can be confidently identified in a character. Dr Kenn acts as the moral centre to the book and his advice to Maggie on the nature of social duty (Book 7, Chapter 2) is the essence of Eliot's own ethical belief.

5.3 VARIETIES OF STYLE

The reader has to be prepared for chameleon changes of style, not only between, for instance, dialectal humour, narration, and reflective analysis, but in the language structures employed. Some paragraphs are of considerable complexity (possibly Eliot was not unaffected by her years translating from German), but in each case the complexity will be found justified by the labyrinthine way in which people's minds actually work. Such a paragraph is the description of Tulliver's reaction to his failure in the law suit where his contradictory actions are explained. His pride is as great as a 'very lofty personage' but his tragedy like that of so many other 'insignificant people' is hidden – he is like those animals who cannot survive the shock of change, so his only possibility of survival lies in refusing to believe in his defeat. The reader is repeatedly involved – 'you perceive the people you pass', and the scope of the paragraph is considerable, moving from Tulliver into history and dramatic tragedy, into ordinary human life and then into animal behaviour, the whole being directed firmly towards our comprehension of just why the miller as he rides back home refuses, with one part of his mind, to admit what has happened. The paragraph is organised with considerable clausal complexity – there are ten dependent clauses in one sentence alone; there is an emphatic doubling of adjectives – 'conspicuous, far echoing', 'worn and disappointed', and a characteristic combination of simple and complex vocabulary.

Typically, the preceding paragraph gave us Tulliver's confused rush of plans and recollections in the very words which would form in his mind and the following paragraph is different again. It is very brief and narrates his visit to St Ogg's coach office to summon Maggie home. Why he does this he cannot admit to himself, and though the author asks the reader for an answer, none is supplied, since the necessary clues have been offered in the complexity of the previous paragraph, a complexity justified by the complication of the way Tulliver's mind is working (Book 3, Chapter 1).

The account of the thoughts tumbling through Tulliver's mind is an example of a technique Eliot often uses called 'erlebte Rede', a German phrase best translated as 'what is passing through the mind' and which is the obvious forerunner of the twentieth-century 'stream of consciousness'. She ceases to give an objective account of the characters' thoughts and instead allows their flow of incomplete and often contradictory impressions to well out in their own particular idiom. Absence of the censorship attached to the spoken word, and the eddying confluence of memories, fears, possibilities, stratagems, not only make the characters credible to us, but often because they are now so vulnerable to the reader's understanding, it arouses that sympathy for their private predicament which is her objective (see section 4.2).

The account of Maggie's flight to the gypsies passes unobtrusively in and out of this style – here is her own voice: 'Everything would be quite charming when she had taught the gypsies to use a washing basin and to feel an interest in books'; and later on 'If her father would but come by in the gig and take her up! Or even if Jack the Giantkiller or Mr Greatheart or St George who slew the dragon on the half-pennies would happen to pass that way' (Book 1, Chapter 11). Everything here bears Maggie's stamp – the 'charming' and 'the dragon on the half-pennies' are as characteristic as her total change of viewpoint about gypsies.

Perhaps we are able to listen in to Maggie's and Mr Tulliver's thoughts more often, but the observant reader will realise that nearly every character can be overheard at times – Bob Jakin longing for his knife back, Mrs Tulliver wondering if she had danced with Wakem in her youth, Lucy's benevolent plans, or Stephen trying not to think about Maggie, as at the end of Book 6, Chapter 6.

Eliot's style is often highly ironic. Sometimes this is sustained over a long passage, as when she reviews 'good society' in Book 4, Chapter 3, but like Jane Austen, she will often put a whole scene or character into perspective by a single flick of irony. This occurs in the final sentence of Book 5, Chapter 2 when Tom's Herculean efforts in raising money are suddenly diminished by: 'Did he not deserve it? He was quite sure that he did.'

Similarly brief are some sentences whose significance can only be seen in retrospect or which pass so swiftly - as in real conversation - that the inattentive reader will hardly notice them. Perhaps we should remember how widespread was the Victorian habit of reading aloud - Eliot's and Lewes's letters are full of such references - and try to slow up our own rate accordingly. An example of the first is the moving and unpointed irony which describes Tom's speech at the creditors' dinner: 'Tom himself got up and made the single speech of his life.' An example of the second comes when Maggie is explaining to Lucy why she would marry Philip: 'I think it would be the best and highest lot for me - to make his life happy. He loved me first. No one else could be quite what he is to me.' Lucy does not think to ask Maggie who loved her second and nor do many readers.

Eliot gives a great deal to her audience - but her complex, varied style requires from them a constant vigilance in return.

5.4 CHARACTER AND PLOT

If a plot, as the novelist E. M. Forster said, is a narrative of events, the emphasis falling on causality, the novelist's concern is to make the causality convincing: what a character does must appear inevitable according to what we have learnt about him. Though chance (more grandly called Fate) can enter at times, too many coincidences, disasters, long-lost heirs, missing wills, shipwrecks or earthquakes will make for melodrama. The reader may well go on enjoying the novel but will no longer believe in, or indeed notice, the characters. Chance does sometimes enter *The Mill on the Floss* - Mrs Pullet's observation of Philip at the Red Deeps, Bob Jakin having a commercially-minded travelling friend and mightily, of course, in the random effects of the great flood. Eliot explicitly notes that the tragedy of our lives is not created entirely from within and points out how well things might have gone with Hamlet if his uncle had died young, but most of the time her plots grow organically from the interaction of character, and in a particular way.

She says of Tom that he was 'like every one of us, imprisoned within the limits of his own nature'. He sees himself in a certain way, but this is not how other characters see him. To take a simple example, Mr Stelling sees him as dull and stupid, Mrs Stelling as obliging and fond of children, Philip as a lumbering idiot, his mother as 'a nice fresh-skinned lad as anybody need wish to see' and there are many other opinions. What is more, character, as Eliot says in *Middlemarch*, 'is a process and an unfolding' and so opinions about him will also change – 'his uncle Deane . . . soon began to conceive hopes of him', 'Maggie had an awe of him, against which she struggled' (Book 5, Chapter 2), Lucy will like him because he gives her a new dog when her old one dies but will then find cause to call him 'awful cousin Tom' (Book 6, Chapter 13). What is true of Tom is true of all the characters in the book. The quality of each character's individuality is shown against the quite different judgements passed by others. The clash between self-estimation and public estimation is presented dramatically, and the resultant friction provides the causality which is the fuel of the plot: Maggie runs off to the gypsies, Mr Tulliver returns Aunt Glegg's loan. Remembering Eliot's remarks about her novels consisting of a 'set of experiments' (section 4.6), the episodes here are startlingly like a series of chemical combinations, under different laboratory conditions. The Tulliver/Wakem and the Maggie/Tom experiments provide explosive combinations. Even Dr Kenn's good opinion of Maggie 'hardens' when it is exposed to the censure of St Ogg's.

Tulliver's motivation in going to law against Pivart provides an illustration. Pivart's lawyer is Wakem and Tulliver sees Wakem like this: 'Wakem's rascality was of that peculiarly aggravated kind which placed itself in opposition to that form of right embodied in Mr Tulliver's interests and opinions'. His view of himself is of an honest upright miller who understands the 'nature of irrigation' – he is therefore justified in entering into conflict with a 'raskell'. Wakem sees Tulliver as a 'hot tempered fellow who would always give you a handle against him – a pitiable furious bull entangled in the meshes of a net'. But the experiment is rarely a simple one-to-one opposition. Tulliver is constantly irritated by the contempt in which Mrs Glegg holds him (since he is so clearly not a Dodson) but his final precipitance into action comes from his wife. She sees her husband as a man who cares more for winning his law case than safeguarding his family. This is definitely not how Mr Tulliver sees himself. Besides, he sees himself as master in his house. In this one single matter (urging him not to go to law) Mrs Tulliver is challenging that image. So, disastrously, he *does* go to law and the whole family suffers irremediable damage.

The discrepancy between the way Tom and Maggie see themselves and the way they see each other is already mapped out in the opening chapters. Tom sees all girls as silly, while Maggie knows she is amazingly clever; Tom knows he is always right while Maggie knows he is 'cruel'. Later on, under the burden of financial responsibility, Tom sees himself as self-sacrificing and admirably hard-working, and so do all the Dodsons, but

Maggie also sees him as 'nothing but a Pharisee'; Philip sees him as 'coarse and narrow-minded'. Maggie is sure her 'reasons of the heart' are good ones but Tom describes her as taking 'ridiculous flights first into one extreme and then into the other'. Finally Tom will refuse even shelter to Maggie, his hatred made more bitter because of the memory of previous fondness and because she brings disgrace to the family – that is, she is damaging Tom's proud image of himself as 'respectable'.

With such continuous jostling of self-images, who needs plots? They grow of themselves, but the novelist has always another problem awaiting him – and that is the problem of ending.

5.5 THE PROBLEM OF ENDING

'Conclusions are the weak point of most authors, but some of the fault lies in the very nature of a conclusion, which is at best a negation', Eliot wrote in an 1857 letter. Her ending to this novel was almost universally criticised. It was felt to be too abrupt, melodramatic, inadequately prepared: 'The story is suddenly carried off its legs in the flood that drowns poor Maggie; and the remaining characters are hustled from the stage at one stroke as if author and readers were alike glad to be rid of them.' This was from the hostile *Dublin University Magazine* of 1861 and the novelist Bulwer Lytton did not believe that Tom could 'be jerked back into the old boyish love of a sudden and we don't see why he should be drowned at all'. Certainly most readers are taken aback by this return to the Maggie/Tom theme after the long Book 6 involvement with Maggie/Stephen, though it is not true that there is no foreshadowing of the end – Maggie has been associated with ideas of water and drowning from the beginning of the novel.

Very soon after its publication, Eliot saw 'the absence of things that might have been there . . . the third volume has the material of a novel compressed into it'. Perhaps she is saying here that the agonised conflict between love and social duty is too easily solved for Maggie by the flood; perhaps she wished for more time to draw the reader's sympathy back to Tom (the suggestions of his love for Lucy are left undeveloped) and to prepare for his new understanding of Maggie just before they are drowned.

The discrepancy between the symbolic treatment of the flood and the psychological realism of human relationships is exemplified by the final sentence of the chapter – the image of Maggie and Tom clasping 'their little hands in love' contradicts the stormy imbalance of the relationship that has been presented so painfully at the beginning of the book. This is how little Maggie would have liked things to be and there is a sense in which the whole of the rescue sequence and specially Tom's sudden change of heart, reads like the 'opium' of Maggie's daydreams when she would 'fancy it was all different, refashioning her little world into just what she should like it to be' (Book 1, Chapter 6).

The conclusion is brevity itself. 'To the eyes that have dwelt on the past, there is no thorough repair' - so perhaps this handful of brief paragraphs stylistically presents a fitting suggestion of damaged fragments which can never be fully restored. Even so, the final inscription can seem curiously inappropriate in relation to the whole novel - and remember the poor drowned woman in Book 1, Chapter 3.

5.6 IMAGES AND REALITY

Rivers

The rivers, Ripple and Floss, are always present in the story, as is the memory of floods. Eliot went to great pains to find a convincing setting, finally chosing Gainsborough in Lincolnshire, near the confluence of the Idle and the Trent. Arbury Mill which she loved as a child provided the details of the great heaps of corn and the floury spiders. Even away from Dorlcote Mill, the rivers are never far distant: both the Glegg and the Deane gardens slope down to the Floss, Bob's house is on the river bank, Guest & Co.'s prosperity stems from the wharves, Maggie's first memory is standing hand in hand with Tom beside the Floss and it is the boating expeditions which lead to the final catastrophe.

Obviously the river holds a multiplicity of symbols. It represents the flow of time, the passage of history and fate. It is the life-giver - the mill depends upon its power - but in flood it becomes the waters of Lethe. For Maggie it has always been the waters whose crossing leads to Paradise (Book 1, Chapter 5).

Places

The Red Deeps, seen only in springtime, carries suggestions of sexual awakening. Dorlcote Mill changes appropriately with the changing fortunes of its inhabitants - the bright fire of its first mention, the delicious cooking smells and Mrs Tulliver's pretty china with its gold sprigs, bleaken into a cheap fire of sticks, coarse food and bare boards. The Deane house, in contrast, seems full of footstools, embroidery and cushions. Aunt Glegg's mildewed mirrors, inquisitive windows and her manipulation of window blinds are as typical of her as the keys, the roomfuls of used physic bottles and the preternatural cleanliness are of Garum Firs.

Maggie's reading

Soon we realise Eliot's economy of technique, for realistic detail often carries further significance. Scott's *The Pirate* has rival fair and dark heroines, thwarted love and shipwreck. Defoe's *History of the Devil* shows an innocent woman drowning and Maggie's proud demonstration of her knowledge of Bunyan to Mr Riley acts as a prologue to the importance of that moral fable for the whole novel. Maggie is haunted by images of Apollyon on her way to the gypsies and then longs for rescue from Mr Greatheart. Like Christiana, she gains spiritual solace in the Valley of Humiliation but at last, like the pilgrims, finds there is no abiding satisfaction in this temporal world.

Music

Eliot loved music and uses it here in a surprising variety of ways. It is used as a plot device, bringing Lucy, Philip, Stephen and Maggie together repeatedly in a special situation which enables one to be watching others and then acting upon that evidence: this is why Philip decides to send Stephen instead of himself on the boat trip.

Attitude to music also acts as a kind of diagnostic of types - Lucy, Philip, Stephen and Maggie delight in it but Tom calls it 'roaring la la' (Book 2, Chapter 4) and the Dodson connection is limited to Uncle Pullet's musical snuff box. Indeed, Tom is seen by Lucy as a threat to their singing because he may forbid Maggie meeting Philip, and he is contemptuous of the Christmas singers (only 'Old Patch, the parish clerk') whereas Maggie connects them with the angels. The Dodson indifference to music extends over the whole of St Ogg society - Lucy knows she cannot find any other singers.

Music is used throughout as a metaphor for Maggie's state of mind. Her 'strangeness' is epitomised for her mother by her habit of singing to herself 'like a Bedlam creature' (Book 1, Chapter 2), she sings for joy when Tom is coming home, her desolation of spirit is instanced specially by the absence of music: 'no piano, no harmonious voices, no delicious stringed instruments . . . sending a strong vibration through her frame' (Book 4, Chapter 3). The effect of Thomas à Kempis is 'as if she had been wakened in the night by a strain of solemn music . . . with much chanting . . . the long lingering vibrations of such a voice' (Book 4, Chapter 3). When she meets Philip again, his song acts like a catalyst, instantly reviving all the romantic yearnings she thought she had lost and her longing to be with him is repeatedly expressed in terms of music - 'like chimes borne onward by a recurrent breeze'.

Finally the use of music both realistically and as a metaphor enables Eliot to elude contemporary censorship concerning sexual attraction. Every detail here is significant: the way Stephen explicitly gives himself and Lucy the personae of 'Adam and Eve unfallen' (in Haydn's *Creation*) before Maggie appears on the scene – Maggie's remark to Lucy that music releases her from 'a weight' (of responsibility?). There is the reiterated use of the word 'vibrate' in reaction to musical sound: Maggie's sensibility to the supreme excitement of music – to her, tunes are 'a pregnant, passionate language'. The effect of Stephen's Masaniello song on her is expressed in words like 'quivering', 'thrill', 'clasping', 'dilated', 'delight', suggesting an intensely sensuous response, as does the surrender of 'strong for all enjoyment, weak for all resistance'. Philip then sings Bellini with a 'pleading tenor' but Maggie is 'touched, not thrilled'; there is 'quiet regret in the place of excitement' (Book 6, Chapter 7). A little later (Chapter 13) music is again used to show Stephen's passion for Maggie: singing 'was a way of speaking to Maggie . . . he was impelled to it by a secret longing, running counter to all his self-confessed resolves, to deepen the hold he had on her'.

The image of music rendering Maggie powerless is then transferred to the powerful tides of the Floss which carry the lovers beyond their conscious control.

6 CRITICAL ANALYSIS

6.1 APPROACH

Every reader must understand what the author is saying, but the student must also be able to identify how the effect is achieved. How does the writer hold and manipulate our attention? How is the narrative forwarded? From whose point of view are we now looking? What do we learn from this passage that alters a previous impression? How is time manipulated? How emotionally involved or how objective are we being made?

With every passage for analysis, different questions are relevant, but basically the questions are two:

1. What would our understanding of the book lack if these paragraphs were missing?

2. By what means does the writer establish this reaction?

It is useful to start by indicating the relationship of the passage to the central concerns of the novel, but this should be both brief and precise. Then, remembering that nothing is included in a novel by chance, but that the author exercises continual selection, ask what this choice of episode intends to do - illustrate, emphasise, demonstrate, counterpoint, hark back or hark forward. Within the episode will be all kinds of other authorial choices and the significance of each must be considered, whether of incident, setting, weather, colour, clothes, who is allowed to be present - in each case ask yourself why the author is selecting and rejecting as she does. Do characters make a significant gesture, or remain oddly silent? What does their manner of speech reveal? Why is the speaker saying this - that is, is he trying to manipulate or deceive - is there a 'subtext'? Such details will build up to establish the emotional mood of the passage without the author having to be explicit - she is 'showing, not telling'.

Sometimes an incident or detail may be of such significance that you realise it has symbolic overtones, as the river does in this novel; sometimes, like music, it can serve several purposes at the same time (see section 5.6). Or a realistic detail may also be an image, as Tulliver's habit of turning his head from side to side.

Notice references, like the ones in this novel to Bunyan, and decide what the author wants them to add to the scene, the images and the exact vocabulary used. Think of the huge lists of synonyms that Roget's *Thesaurus* offers - why then does the author select this particular word? Even proper names are carefully chosen. Look at the order of words in sentences - inversion, for instance, is there to serve a purpose and the length of sentences and structure of a paragraph may both be significant.

Continually ask, who is speaking here? Eliot is particularly skilful at slipping in and out of a character's mind, even during a sentence. Sometimes a glance at punctuation helps - a series of loose phrases connected with dashes may suggest emotional stress. Remember that a dramatist can depend on actors to add tone and significance to the text of a play, but the novelist has to use language to make the reader hear in the right way.

Look out, too, for irony. Eliot often uses it and depends on her reader to recognise the possible alternatives irony always suggests. Every passage is different - what we have to do is to obey Henry James: 'Be one of those upon whom nothing is lost'.

6.2 SPECIMEN PASSAGE AND CRITICAL COMMENTARY

Specimen passage

Two hours ago, as Tom was walking to St Ogg's, he saw the distant future before him, as he might have seen a tempting stretch of smooth sandy beach beyond a belt of flinty shingles: he was on the grassy bank then, and thought the shingles might soon be passed. But now his feet were on the sharp stones: the belt of shingles had widened, and the stretch of sand had dwindled into narrowness.

'What did my uncle Deane say, Tom?' said Maggie, putting her arm through Tom's as he was warming himself rather drearily by the kitchen fire. 'Did he say he would give you a situation?'

'No, he didn't say that. He didn't quite promise me anything: he seemed to think I couldn't have a very good situation. I'm too young.'

'But didn't he speak kindly, Tom?'

'Kindly? Pooh! what's the use of talking about that? I wouldn't care about his speaking kindly if I could get a situation. But it's such a nuisance and bother - I've been at school all this while learning Latin and things - not a bit of good to me - and now my uncle says I must set about learning book-keeping and calculation and those things. He seems to make out I'm good for nothing.'

Tom's mouth twitched with a bitter expression as he looked at the fire.

'O what a pity we haven't got Dominie Sampson,' said Maggie, who couldn't help mingling some gaiety with their sadness. 'If he had taught me book-keeping by double entry and after the Italian method, as he did Lucy Bertram. I could teach you, Tom.'

'*You* teach! Yes, I daresay. That's always the tone you take,' said Tom.

'Dear Tom! I was only joking,' said Maggie, putting her cheek against his coat sleeve.

'But it's always the same, Maggie,' said Tom, with the little frown he put on when he was about to be justifiably severe. 'You're always setting yourself up above me and every one else. And I've wanted to tell you about it several times. You ought not to have spoken as you did to my uncles and aunts - you should leave it to me to take care of my mother and you, and not put yourself forward. You think you know better than any one, but you're almost always wrong. I can judge much better than you can.'

Poor Tom! he had just come from being lectured and made to feel his inferiority: the reaction of his strong, self-asserting nature must take place somehow, and here was a case in which he could justly show himself dominant. Maggie's cheek flushed and her lip quivered with conflicting resentment and affection and a certain awe as well as admiration of Tom's firmer and more effective character. She did not answer immediately; very angry words rose to her lips, but they were driven back again, and she said at last,

'You often think I'm conceited, Tom, when I don't mean what I say at all in that way. I don't mean to put myself above you - I know you behaved better than I did yesterday. But you are always so harsh to me, Tom.'

With the last words the resentment was rising again.

'No, I'm not harsh,' said Tom, with severe decision. 'I'm always kind to you; and so I shall be: I shall always take care of you. But you must mind what I say.'

Their mother came in now, and Maggie rushed away, that her burst of tears, which she felt must come, might not happen till she was safe upstairs. They were very bitter tears: everybody in the world seemed so hard and unkind to Maggie: there was no indulgence, no fondness, such as she imagined when she fashioned the world afresh in her own thoughts. In books there were people who were always agreeable or tender, and delighted to do things that made one happy, and who did not show their kindness by finding fault. The world outside the books was not a happy one, Maggie felt: it seemed to be a world where people behaved the best to those they did not pretend to love and that did not belong to them. And if life had no love in it, what else was there for Maggie? Nothing but poverty and the companionship of her mother's narrow griefs - perhaps of her father's heart-cutting childish dependence. There is no hopelessness so sad as that of early youth, when the soul is made up of wants, and has no long memories, no superadded life in the life of others; though we who look on think lightly of such premature despair, as if our vision of the future lightened the blind sufferer's present.

Maggie in her brown frock with her eyes reddened and her heavy hair pushed back, looking from the bed where her father lay, to the dull walls of this sad chamber which was the centre of her world, was a creature full of eager, passionate longings for all that was beautiful and glad: thirsty for all knowledge: with an ear straining after dreamy music that died away and would not come near to her: with a blind, unconscious yearning for something that would link together the wonderful impressions of this mysterious life and give her soul a sense of home in it.

No wonder, when there is this contrast between the outward and the inward, that painful collisions come of it. A girl of no startling appearance, and who will never be a Sappho or a Madame Roland or anything else that the world takes wide note of, may still hold forces within her as the living plant-seed does, which will make a way for themselves, often in a shattering, violent manner. (Book 3, Chapter 5. The final paragraph, present in the manuscript, was not printed in early editions.)

Critical commentary

Tom's hopeful plan of rescuing the Tulliver fortunes by getting a job has received a set-back since Uncle Deane is by no means as confident as Tom that he would be a useful employee. Tom has returned from his interview and Maggie is anxious to hear what has happened. The episode that follows shows how the incompatibility of Tom and Maggie is being made worse as the reality of their situation is forced upon them and illusion evaporates.

Both, by the end of the episode are 'bitter' but while Tom's reaction comes from the damage done to his self-image, since his uncle 'seems to make out I'm good for nothing', and the shock of harsh reality - 'I couldn't have a very good situation', the adjective revealing his high hopes, Maggie's misery comes from Tom's coldness for 'if life had no love in it, what else was there for Maggie?' Tom broods bitterly upon the unexpected repulse to his ambition but to Maggie, Tom is more important than the outside world and she offers him 'gaiety' and gestures of loving affection (her arm through Tom's, her cheek against his sleeve). She is principally concerned whether their uncle has spoken 'kindly' and this word is then tossed between them in a revealing way. Tom repeats it twice, with contemptuous exclamation: 'Kindly? Pooh! what's the use . . . I wouldn't care about his speaking kindly'. He vents his resentment on Maggie but when she complains he is 'always so harsh', he paradoxically claims to be 'always kind', and in the emphatic monosyllables which follow identifies his concept of kindness as guardianship and authority: ' . . . you must mind what I say'. To Maggie, however, a world where people only 'show their kindness by finding fault' (like Aunt Glegg) brings 'premature despair'.

Tom's reaction to 'being lectured' by his uncle is to reassert his authority where he can, and his language bears the stamp of his 'strong self-asserting nature' – often monosyllabic, simple, short-sentenced, full of 'I – you' antitheses and of obligatory verbs – 'ought', 'should', 'must'. The language surrounding him is equally 'harsh' – he is associated in the first image of his disappointment with 'sharp stones' and the thrice-repeated 'shingles', even fire cannot warm him except 'drearily', he has the 'frown' he had tried to assume when he had terrified Maggie with Poulter's sword, and words like 'severe' (twice), 'justly', 'dominant' 'firmer', 'decision', are used of him. No wonder by the end Maggie's 'lip quivered' as Tom's had 'twitched' earlier on.

But 'Poor Tom' says Eliot, and the balance between the two is fairly kept. He is 'too young' as Uncle Deane has said and he has only just discovered that the education so painfully endured is 'not a bit of good'. Eliot emphasises that his nature 'must' react (as we will later be told Maggie's will). His judgement that Maggie's outburst to the aunts was useless is correct and his determination to 'always take care of you' is admirable. Besides, Maggie's reference to a novel Tom almost certainly had not read would irritate him and by now she should realise he does not understand a 'joke'. Maggie has a 'certain awe' of his nature but the phrase 'conflicting resentment and affection' sums up their relationship.

The first half of the episode presents the tension between the two dramatically, the language, gestures and facial expressions of each illustrating their opposed temperaments, but then we follow Maggie upstairs to 'the centre of her world'. Dialogue is now balanced by narration, and the weight of sympathy swings to Maggie. Tom has been left with his mother and though he is bitterly disappointed, there is a path ahead if he learns 'book-keeping and calculations and those things' (the vagueness of the last is typical of Tom's inarticulacy and youth). Moreover, his vision of the future, in the vivid image with which this passage starts, has become difficult but not impossible – the 'stretch of sand had dwindled' but not vanished. For Maggie, since she is a woman, the future is bleaker. The books she relies on for her 'opium' have misled her, and here her own language shows through – 'in books there were people who . . . delighted to do things that made one happy'. She has suffered Tom's harshness and the phrases about her parents are equally painful – her mother's 'narrow griefs' and her father's 'heart-cutting' dependence. At this point the reader's own experience is dovetailed into the novel by the use of 'we' and 'our' with an ironic reminder of the genuine pain of adolescent despair. Maggie's 'hopelessness' is now caught in a sombre visual image – 'brown frock', 'eyes reddened', 'heavy hair' and this seeps over to her surroundings – 'dull walls of this sad chamber', a picture made more painful by the contrast between this outer life and the 'passionate longings . . . yearnings' which Maggie cannot even identify and which are imaged (typically in this novel) as music she cannot quite hear.

The final paragraphs broaden from Maggie's particular plight to the frustrations of many ordinary women – 'a creature . . . a girl' in her society, and with another powerful image, this time drawn from plant-life, Eliot suggests their potential explosiveness. The tone of rational foreboding is underlined by the reference to women who may have died violently because of an alien society.

The episode shows how Tulliver's sudden ruin has affected the children. Both are being made to face an unpleasant reality which neither is yet mature enough to meet. Tom looks forward uneasily to a difficult and uncongenial future and Maggie sees Tom changed from the belovèd brother of her imagination and lacks even the meagre expectations that his more active male role offers.

7 CRITICAL RECEPTION

7.1 CONTEMPORARY REVIEWS AND REACTIONS [quotations of early reviews come from *George Eliot: the Critical Heritage*, ed. David Carroll (Routledge & Kegan Paul, 1971)]

Adam Bede had been a great success (Queen Victoria had commissioned paintings of episodes from the story) and *The Mill on the Floss* rode on the crest of this popularity, selling 6000 copies in seven weeks, but soon came a reaction and both the second and third editions hung fire. Reasons quite extraneous to the novel itself contributed to this hesitation: between the two novels the identity of the writer had been revealed and this carried three causes of scandal. The author was a woman; she was living with a man not her husband; she was recognised as the translator of a book challenging the historical basis of Christianity. Some of the early reviews are coloured by their unease with this unconventional lady.

Particularly admired was the ability to portray real children with their conflicting passions, such as Maggie 'full of affection' but first introduced to us driving a nail into her doll's head. Critics also praised the way Eliot showed her characters being worked on alike by environment, family traits and genetic pattern, the 'analysis of the interior life of the mind', the ability to make characters speak for themselves and show slight but significant differences of personality, and the undercurrent of symbolism: 'Even in the material facts (is) a half-hidden symbolism'. Some admired how 'naturally and powerfully' the love between men and women was expressed and nearly all, the imaginative power of Maggie's creation.

There was, however, adverse critical comment upon the structure, characterisation, subject matter and moral tone of the novel. Complaints were made about the 'dislocation . . . between Maggie's girlhood and the great temptation'; that with the last volume, the reader 'passes into a new book'; that the first two volumes constituted a 'masterly fragment of fictitious biography' followed by a second-rate one-volume novel. The crisis was considered as two sudden and too violent. The death of Maggie and Tom left too many questions unanswered and the reader unsatisfied. The characterisation of Maggie was judged inconsistent: 'the young woman with the overmastering passion is very slightly connected with the little Maggie of the Mill'. A different kind of criticism disliked having characters like the Dodsons – 'stingy, selfish wretches' – and as bigoted as Tom. Yet others felt Eliot was unjust in showing 'disdain' for Tom. Characters, theme, setting and plot were felt to be repellently realistic – 'examples taken from the meanest, poorest and grossest types of human character'. The delineation of the mutual passion between Stephen and Maggie was deprecated – 'it is not consistent with female delicacy to lay so much stress on the bodily feelings of the other sex'. The poet Swinburne felt Stephen should be horse-whipped for admiring Maggie's arms and a Dublin reviewer could not credit that a 'woman of Maggie's sort' could love the 'sweet-voiced coxcomb, Stephen Guest'. Some reviewers were uneasy because they could not identify the moral centre of the book. Dr Kenn was felt to be 'faded' and there was no source of pithy country wisdom like Mrs Poyser in *Adam Bede*. Instead the reader was left in moral uncertainty, since the sympathy Eliot demanded for her characters pointed in different directions from conventionally accepted principles. Besides, the web of heredity and circumstance was so strongly woven that the characters seemed to be left with no free will to choose 'right or wrong . . . fate is triumphant not only against human happiness but against human virtue.'

The justice of some criticisms Eliot acknowledged, agreeing that 'the tragedy is not adequately prepared'. Her explanation was that her love for the subject of the early books, Maggie and Tom as children and growing up, had 'beguiled' her into a generously full treatment which unbalanced the novel. Why she had written about such ordinary people she felt she had dealt with in the book itself (Book 4, Chapter 1), but she was taken aback by the general dislike for the Dodsons and Tom. She deals succinctly with the *Macmillan's Magazine's* April 1861 criticism that she had not appreciated Tom's sterling qualities and enquires how the reviewer 'would have respected Tom if I had not painted him with respect? . . . Tom is painted with as much love and pity as Maggie'. Criticism of Maggie's love for Stephen she will not admit. She wrote to her publisher:

> If I am wrong there I ought not to have written this book at all . . . If the ethics of art do not admit the truthful presentation of a character essentially noble but liable to great error . . . then . . . the ethics of art are too narrow and should be widened to correspond with a widening psychology.

7.2 SUBSEQUENT HISTORY OF THE BOOK

In spite of some dissatisfied voices, the novel's popularity was soon established - it was thought to have the charm, humour and pathos of a vanishing country and provincial life. With *Silas Marner* it became a useful Sunday School prize, and was regarded well into this century as a suitable schoolroom text for thirteen-year-olds, curiously placed beside the anodyne mildness of *Essays of Elia* by Charles Lamb or Robert Louis Stevenson's *Travels with a Donkey*. Attitudes of the general reading public and the literary critic, however, underwent what David Cecil called a 'catastrophic slump' after her death. Though this is not unusual, for Dickens suffered a similar critical (but not popular) disdain until the mid-1940s, Eliot's was so marked that Gerald Bullet in his 1946 biography said her figure had not only fallen from its pedestal but had been 'swept away in fragments by the janitor'.

One reason for this disfavour may have been the lifeless and heavily censored biography published by her husband, John Cross, in 1885. The image that emerged from this was of a gloomy, over-intellectual moralist and the impression seeped over into the estimate of her novels. These were now criticised for lack of form, humourlessness, intrusive authorial comment and for a didactic purpose that deformed her real creative genius, so that her characters were seen as puppets manipulated to illustrate a thesis.

Such views were challenged by the novelist and critic Virginia Woolf in 1919. She particularly admired the stimulating way Eliot's voice is heard in her novels - she 'was compelled by the very power of her genius to step forth in person upon the quiet bucolic scene'. Indeed, Virginia Woolf suggested that the reason for much of the adverse criticism was that most critics were men, and expected women to write books of a particular kind. The rural charm of *Adam Bede* was found admirable, but they were ill at ease when Eliot moved on to the far less comfortable themes of her later novels. It was not until after the Second World War that she was reinstated as one of the greatest writers of English novels, with *Middlemarch* widely acknowledged as her supreme work. Interestingly, contemporary critical opinion of *The Mill on the Floss* in many respects resembles that of its first enthusiastic reviewers, though no one now challenges the likelihood of the Maggie/Stephen relationship. There is unreserved admiration for the picture of the children, for her psychological realism, independent moral perception, ironic humour and ability to present characters dramatically - and there is still considerable critical debate about the providential flood.

REVISION QUESTIONS

1. Contemporary critics complained that Maggie would never have fallen in love with a man like Stephen Guest, but Eliot was convinced it was 'a vital part of my whole conception and purpose'. Give the case on both sides.
2. There was considerable discussion between publisher, writer and her friends over this novel's title. What elements in the novel justify the final choice? Is is unsuitable in any respects?
3. Eliot is often praised for her intense awareness of the process of change. Discuss.
4. Dislike of Tom and excessive indulgence towards Maggie are common modern responses – they are also wrong responses. Do you agree?
5. *The Mill on the Floss* can be seen as a critique of the assumption of male superiority. What evidence is there for or against this?
6. The humour and compassion with which Eliot presents Maggie's childhood and adolescence are lacking in the latter part of the novel. Discuss whether this is true, and if so what qualities replace them?
7. Critics complained that the death of Maggie and Tom left too many questions unanswered and the reader unsatisfied. Is this criticism justified?
8. Eliot has been described as 'a natural scientist who judges and loves the specimens'. Demonstrate what this means in terms of two of the main and two of the minor characters of *The Mill on the Floss*.
9. Eliot's genius lies in the understanding of passion. Discuss this in relation to all four Tullivers.
10. How important is money in this novel?
11. Select three characters who are shown from different points of view and discuss how this also throws light on the character whose viewpoint we temporarily share.
12. 'In every novel . . . there are "chorus parts" which create for the reader a sense of the animated human environment in which this particular drama moves.' Show how this applies to *The Mill on the Floss*.

FURTHER READING

Biography and background

M. Laski, *George Eliot and her World* (Thames & Hudson, 1973)
G. S. Haight, *George Eliot: a Biography* (Oxford University Press, 1968)
G. S. Haight (ed.), *Selected Letters of George Eliot* (Yale University Press, 1985)
R. Redinger, *George Eliot: The Emergent Self* (Bodley Head, 1975)
B. Willey, *Nineteenth-Century Studies: Coleridge to Matthew Arnold* (Chatto & Windus, 1949)

Criticism

J. Bennett, *George Eliot: Her Mind and Art* (Cambridge University Press, 1948)
D. Carroll (ed.), *George Eliot: The Critical Heritage* (Routledge & Kegan Paul, 1971)
B. Hardy (ed.), *Critical Essays on George Eliot* (Routledge & Kegan Paul, 1970)
W. J. Harvey, *The Art of George Eliot* (Chatto & Windus, 1960)

Text

The edition of *The Mill on the Floss* edited by A. S. Byatt (Penguin English Library, 1979) has been used.